Spiritual CONNECTIONS

OTHER BOOKS BY SYLVIA BROWNE

Adventures of a Psychic (with Antoinette May)
Astrology Through a Psychic's Eyes
Blessings from the Other Side (with Lindsay Harrison)
Contacting Your Spirit Guide (book-with-CD)
Conversations with the Other Side
Exploring the Levels of Creation
Father God
The Healing Journey (available March 2009)
If You Could See What I See
A Journal of Love and Healing (with Nancy Dufresne)
Life on the Other Side (with Lindsay Harrison)
Meditations
Mother God
Mystical Traveler (available September 2008)
The Other Side and Back (with Lindsay Harrison)
Past Lives, Future Healing (with Lindsay Harrison)
Prayers
Prophecy (with Lindsay Harrison)
Secrets & Mysteries of the World
Secret Societies . . . and How They Affect Our Lives Today
Sylvia Browne's Book of Angels
Sylvia Browne's Book of Dreams (with Lindsay Harrison)
Sylvia Browne's Lessons for Life
Temples on the Other Side
Visits from the Afterlife (with Lindsay Harrison)

The Journey of the Soul Series
(available individually or in a boxed set)

God, Creation, and Tools for Life (Book 1)
Soul's Perfection (Book 2)
The Nature of Good and Evil (Book 3)

♛ ♛ ♛

All of the above are available at your
local bookstore, or may be ordered by visiting:

Hay House USA: **www.hayhouse.com**®
Hay House Australia: **www.hayhouse.com.au**
Hay House UK: **www.hayhouse.co.uk**
Hay House South Africa: **www.hayhouse.co.za**
Hay House India: **www.hayhouse.co.in**

Spiritual CONNECTIONS

How to Find Spirituality Throughout All the Relationships in Your Life

SYLVIA BROWNE

HAY HOUSE, INC.
Carlsbad, California • New York City
London • Sydney • Johannesburg
Vancouver • Hong Kong • New Delhi

Published and distributed in the United States by: Hay House, Inc.: www.
hayhouse.com • *Published and distributed in Australia by:* Hay House
Australia Pty. Ltd.: www.hayhouse.com.au • *Published and distributed in the
United Kingdom by:* Hay House UK, Ltd.: www.hayhouse.co.uk • *Published
and distributed in the Republic of South Africa by:* Hay House SA (Pty), Ltd.:
www.hayhouse.co.za • *Distributed in Canada by:* Raincoast: www.raincoast.com
• *Published in India by:* Hay House Publishers India: www.hayhouse.co.in

Editorial supervision: Jill Kramer • *Design:* Tricia Breidenthal

Library of Congress Cataloging-in-Publication Data

Browne, Sylvia.
   Spiritual connections : how to find spirituality throughout all the
relationships in your life / Sylvia Browne. -- 1st ed.
     p. cm.
   ISBN-13: 978-1-4019-0881-2 (hardcover)
   ISBN-13: 978-1-4019-0882-9 (tradepaper)
   1. Interpersonal relations--Religious aspects.   I. Title.
BL626.33.B76 2007
131--dc22

                                                                    2006026943

Tradepaper ISBN: 978-1-4019-0882-9
Hardcover ISBN: 978-1-4019-0881-2

11 10 09 08   6 5 4 3
1st edition, March 2007
3rd edition, May 2008

Printed in the United States of America

To Gina and Nancy
and my precious grandchildren;
to all those I love, have loved, and will love;
and for all of you who have reciprocated—
God bless you, everyone.

CONTENTS

INTRODUCTION

There have been so many self-help books for relationships written over the years, on topics ranging from "how to have a better sex life" to "how to stay married" and even "how to get a friendly divorce." Yet I haven't seen a single volume on how to have a spiritual relationship with the different people in our lives. Nor have I seen any that approach our lives from our own charts' learning processes. Consequently, in *Spiritual Connections,* I've chosen to incorporate some of my own experiences, my years of doing readings, and how our life themes dictate the types of relationships we have.

You meet countless people in a lifetime (or many lifetimes), and this book will explain how each one has an effect on your life. You see, when you wrote your chart before you came into this life, you documented every detail about every encounter . . . no matter how fleeting, aggravating, or toxic it may have seemed. So in this book, I'll take you through each relationship—from family, friends, and lovers to enemies, co-workers, schoolmates, and even God—that creates a ladder to your evolvement. I assure you that you'll never look at other people (and life) in the same way again.

Yes, there are those who will try your patience, but the lessons they give you actually light your way, making it easier for you to get through this lifetime and to the Other Side. Each individual you encounter is like a stepping-stone . . . it's how you handle him or her that determines your advancement. I've even said at lectures that people make us sick or they can make us well . . . but we can always learn something.

In the pages that follow, I'll illuminate just how you're connecting spiritually to each and every person you encounter. In Part I, I'll skim over all of the relationships most of us have so you can see just how many souls you're interacting with on a daily basis. (And I'll offer you a few tidbits of advice that I've picked up over the years, which should help you deal with these individuals.) Then in Part II, I'll look closely at the life themes each of us possesses, in order to help you understand why some relationships have been great for you while others have not.

So roll up your sleeves, take the plunge, and get ready to tackle this life's complicated puzzle. In the process, I hope you'll see that, like many of the things we've made so hard, it's actually quite simple spiritually.

👑 👑 👑

PART I

Whom Are We Connecting With?

Chapter One

THOSE WE ENCOUNTER
FROM DAY TO DAY

I'd like to begin this book by focusing on those people whom you might not consider "important," yet who do factor in much of your day-to-day existence. I call these individuals "our dear facilitators." These include people such as your mechanic, manicurist, barber or hairdresser, butcher, favorite waitress or maître d', travel agent, taxi or limo driver, gardener, plumber, painter, pest-control person, service technician, postal carrier, bank teller, housekeeper, grocery clerk, doctor, dentist, and many more who help out in your life. Don't forget the chimney sweep, veterinarian, dog groomer, jeweler . . . and on and on it goes. All of these individuals make your life easier and are too often taken for granted.

Even if you can't personally relate to the people I'm about to describe, hopefully you'll be able to identify with some of the souls who cross *my* path every day. Take my hairdresser, for instance. His name is Isaac, and I've been with him for 12 years. No, I'm not naturally blonde; my hair is actually a strange maroon color that is *not* attractive, so I have it dyed. I've been with Isaac through the birth of his first child, and we've commiserated over our mutual divorces. We share tidbits about mutual acquaintances, our respective travels, and our families.

Similarly, I see my manicurist of 13 years every two weeks or so. And yes, my nails *are* real. My high school yearbook even stated that "Sylvia will be the most likely to succeed with the longest nails"! Anyway, my manicurist and I love to talk and laugh, but she is supporting her son alone, which can be difficult. One day when she was rubbing my hands, I held on to hers and said, "Everything will be all right this year, and I love you." She had to stop because she started to cry, and when I left, she gave me the biggest hug.

Then there's a special seafood place where I love to eat. When I come in, the owner grabs me and asks how I am, and we talk about his family. There's also a little Italian restaurant where this one waitress (no matter how hot and harassed she is) always runs up to hug me—and it never fails that she gives me an extra meatball! It's like Laura at Gioia (the little dress shop in Santa Monica I go to whenever I'm in the Los Angeles area), who holds things back that she thinks I'll like. She recently bought a house by the sea and is happy with her life now.

I share a gardener with my psychic son Chris. As this man cuts my grass and tends my flowers, I often go out and chat with him. We talk a lot about how you have to keep going in this life. He's smart and wise and wounded (as we all are), but we smile when we see each other.

Then there are others, like Sylvester my sound man, who has been with me for years and helps me when I'm on the road; or Joe, my friend who fixes my TV. After he installed a new DVD player for me awhile back, I asked what I owed him. He smiled and said, "This one's on me!" These kinds of people are woven into the tapestry of our existence . . . and sometimes they're the very ones we take for granted.

My grandmother used to hum a tune that went, "Love the shoemaker, the butcher, the baker, and the candlestick maker, and love will come back to you." I used to think, *What a silly little song,* and *Just who was the candlestick maker?* But that wasn't the point—she was merely reminding me that love comes in many forms.

Love Is All Around Us

Take a moment to think about all the individuals who fill your life. With the world populated by billions of people, each of whom have meaning and significance, how can we be lonely? Yet we live in such a fast-paced society that we don't have time for the grocer or the clerk at our favorite shop. We have no downtime at all anymore. What happened to family meetings, talking at dinner, or going on rides together? Even when we take vacations, we want to have such a good time and try to get everything done that we come home worn out and even crankier than before we left.

This hectic and stressed environment has often caused us to miss out on the joys of one another. For example, I was sitting at a Starbucks the other day having a cup of coffee and enjoying the first smells of spring, when I couldn't help but overhear a conversation between a man and a woman nearby.

She said, "You never pay attention to me anymore."

He answered, "Yes, I do, but you're so needy that I just can't be what you want."

"Then I don't want you," she replied.

I was curious to know if she actually knew what she wanted or if he even had tried to figure it out. And as

simplistic as this sounds, I wondered if things would have been different if they had simply sat there holding hands and enjoying their drinks.

We hear so much about communication—and yes, it *is* important—but sometimes I think that there's too much of what I call "stress verbiage." In other words, most of the time we don't say what we mean, or we expect everyone else to read our minds and break down our barriers.

Ask yourself the following: When was the last time you really laughed? And when was the last time you woke up and wondered what joys the day would bring? I know that life can wear us down to the point that we feel flat and round, just sitting in the stream of life, yet we lose our passion because we forget the meaning of spirituality and how each person we interact with every day shapes our lives. Whether we realize it or not, we borrow or take from those we meet, hopefully keeping the good and trashing the bad. Throughout all of our lives, we've gained knowledge or experience from everyone we've come in contact with, yet we still keep our core personality.

If we lose that essence of ourselves or give our power away, then we're going to become depressed and flounder. If we become too identified with another person, we'll lose ourselves, causing us to be filled with futility. No wonder we have such a tired and depressed society. In my lectures, readings, and TV appearances, I tend to ask if people feel more depressed and worn out these days, and usually thousands of people raise their hands. We've become a culture that doesn't communicate, and we're afraid to show or say what we feel for fear of being branded as weak, stupid, or just crazy.

We've lost so much of that spiritual love that we should be directing toward every human we encounter.

I believe that this is a direct result of our harried society, because I know things weren't always this way. For example, I fondly remember Al, our ice man (this was long before refrigerators). When I was a young girl, my friends and I would run after him, and he'd laughingly chip off a chunk for us—on those steamy Missouri days, that was the best treat in the world. I can still see his grin and his sparkling blue eyes, along with how much pleasure it gave him to be the "king of the ice wagon" and dispense his frozen slivers of refreshment to hot but grateful kids.

By the same token, my father started out as a mailman, and he would come home at Christmas laden with ties, chocolates, and whiskey (even though he didn't drink)—all gifts from the people he'd befriended on his route. Later he became a vice president of one of the largest truck lines in Kansas City, but he never forgot about the man who did his shirts or the grocer who gave him the best cut of meat. And when he heard that our mailman had fallen on hard times, Daddy brought me along to deliver groceries and a Christmas tree to him. Unfortunately, I had to hold the tree outside of the car window, and it was so cold that I felt as if my fingers would fall off. My father looked over at me and, seeing my discomfort, said, "Sylvia, don't think about the cold—just think about the warmth that we're going to bring to the hearts of this family." I swear before God that my fingers magically did become warm.

Many years later when I was teaching at St. Martin's in Sunnyvale, California, two nuns and I would go out every Monday to visit the sick or elderly. Those dear faces were immeasurably filled with love and joy.

All of the people I've described in this chapter, along with those I haven't, are involved in loving, spiritual

relationships with us. They're what make our hearts sing—no, it's not that heart-pounding hormonal lift, but a different type of euphoria. I'm sure it's what is too often lightly called "grace," which is actually God's love descending upon us. This gift gets us out of the whole tiring syndrome of "What about me?"—which is a door that locks us into ourselves and our own so-called misery.

So right now, I want you to stop and think about all the individuals who make you happy, along with those whom *you* make happy. If the answer is no one, then you'd better get out and start loving your fellow men and women. After all, you don't have to be *in* love . . . *to* love.

♛ ♛ ♛

Chapter Two

PEOPLE AT SCHOOL
AND ON THE JOB

*I*n this chapter, I'll be taking a look at relationships we have with those at school and work. Strangely, they can actually set the tempo for the future as much as our home life does (and I'll tackle that topic in the next chapter).

Teachers and Schoolmates

School is a microcosm of life in the sense that how we begin to feel about ourselves in the early years carries over into our adulthood. Sometimes if we're popular in school and then discover that the real world doesn't care that we were the prom queen or basketball star, we can be in for a sad awakening. On the other hand, if we felt like a nerd or an outsider, this can cause us to carry over a feeling of being left out or made fun of, and then we retreat. In other words, these are truly formative years.

Having been a teacher as well as a student, I've seen both sides. When I was in school, I wasn't shy and had quite a temper, especially when I witnessed any type of injustice. I was a good student, but I never felt challenged until I got to college. Since I was usually bored, I wouldn't sit in my seat, and I talked a lot. Yet my sense of humor always saved me, along with the belief that my grandmother instilled in me that God loves everyone (including me). I thought that made a lot of sense, even though I surely didn't like Freddy, who tortured me through grade school and chased me home every day in high school . . . that is, until I broke an umbrella over his back. I'm not violent, but enough is enough!

However, it *is* best to be kind and respectful to our fellow students, for we can form real relationships that last a lifetime. Cliques were certainly around in my day, but all of the people I grew up with got jobs, had families, and didn't end up in jail. Perhaps it was a different world then, but respect, honor, studying hard, and forming a feeling of community and togetherness are timeless qualities.

If you didn't come away with such feelings from your school years, maybe it would behoove you to go back and reconstruct what you would have done differently as a student and implement it into your life now. Maybe you really weren't liked—perhaps you dressed oddly, your hair wasn't right, or you had a horrible case of acne—but then is then and now is now, so let the past be buried. Take what you learned and let it enhance your spirituality, not detract from it.

―◄◘►―

It's important to note that if we're tuned in, many teachers can become mentors or role models for us. For example, I dearly recall my English teacher in college, Sister Marcella Marie. Just to walk into her classroom was a joy—unlike the other nuns, she had flowers and statues around, and she made her room cozy and beautiful. She had such a Divine spark and had no trouble talking about the social, religious, or sexual mores of literature. I loved her so much because she was kind and found blessings even in the darkest dramas. She was the second person (besides my grandmother) who gave me a love of the written word and revealed the power it carried.

Sister Marcella Marie encouraged me to write; and although I didn't complete my first book until I was 49, I did win many awards over the years, including the Golden Echo award in poetry and a national essay contest. She'd always say, "Write how you feel, and feel what you write." She's also the person who made me believe that I could be a pretty good teacher myself someday.

The relationships I had with the students I taught for more than 18 years are also a part of my heart, and I will always cherish them. Every fall I'd tell myself that I wouldn't get so close or plugged in to those kids, but every year they became like my own. I painfully remember how mothers would have to pull their sobbing little ones off me at the end of the last term. Even though I'd be a wreck for a month afterward, I wouldn't have traded that pure love for anything in the world.

I received a letter recently from a doctor whom I'd taught when he was in the fourth grade. It simply said, "I am who I am because you believed in me when I felt like a nerd." It's experiences like this that keep me going.

Now this doesn't mean that you *have* to be a wonderful and great mentor, for you can't fool children. They know if you love them—and if you don't, you shouldn't be working with them—but I certainly formed strong relationships with my students. In fact, when I returned to Kansas City for a lecture many years after I'd left, there were three rows of my third-graders in attendance. And the high-school students I taught have kept in touch with me since the 1960s. These men and women have given me so much love over the years, and they've added so much color and flavor to my life.

At the Workplace

Now let's explore the relationships we have with others on the job, since they can either be really great or hellish. It seems that every day I hear people say that they work in an environment that's too political or commercial, or their employers are only out to cheat or scam others for the almighty dollar. When you find yourself in such a place, I don't think that any amount of security should step on the dignity of your God-center. I don't mean that you have to go around preaching and trying to bend people to your way spiritually, but there is such a thing as honest behavior with integrity. I don't think that anyone is stupid enough not to eventually get the picture when there are bad business practices going on.

And let's say that you're in a situation with a boss who's unreasonable, demanding, egocentric, and restrictive . . . not to mention that the people around you are probably either completely terrified or stepping on each other to get approval from this person, who seems to wield a hammer over everyone's economic status. Well, when you're in this state of never winning, it's time to leave. Not only will the negativity you're encountering on a daily basis spread like a cancer, but no one can bond together if they're living in fear.

Yes, it's true: If you can't stand your job, the resulting stress can *definitely* make you ill. And what is worth that? I know you'll say, "But if I don't have a job, I'll go bankrupt or have to live on the street." No you won't. Remember that Jesus essentially said that God takes care of us just like lilies in a field. It's much better to scale down and be happy than to live your life in a negative and harmful environment. And leaving your job is certainly cheaper than ending up in the hospital, unable to work at all.

On the other hand, as an employee, you owe your company fairness and industriousness—you're also obliged to do things right, take on responsibility, and be innovative. It's amazing to me to watch people continually just do step A without ever advancing to step B. Do your job, but also see what you can do to improve it. By your own reasoning, you'll get to the next step. I hate to say this, but so many times I see individuals who really don't want to work. So you give them something to do, but they simply can't get it right. It's almost as if they're frozen in their own insecurity or inability to see "outside the box." Again, just as the boss must be fair, so must the employee be fair by trying to do his or her best. To love your job, you have to love what you do—this doesn't just mean the paycheck, but rather being proud of yourself for what you're accomplishing.

That line "Can't we all just get along!" sounds corny and even humorous, but it's so true. You don't have to love everyone (or even like them), but if your co-workers are doing a good job, it's all right to leave them alone rather than taking out your dislike on them and others. An office is another microcosm of the universe, and whether it's easy or hard, you still learn. Plus, what does

love cost? Nothing. However, hate, jealousy, and vengeance take a lot from you because God is love and we're His genetic offspring. Loving each other is part of our spiritual DNA.

Nevertheless, I do know how difficult these interpersonal situations can be. When I taught, I got caught up in a situation in which a PE teacher and a nun who taught literature just couldn't stand me. I agonized over this until one day when one of my students came to see me while I was grading papers. She sat down, looked in my eyes, and said, "You know why those two women hate you? It's because we all [meaning the students] love you so much."

I thought about that for a long time and was totally confused. I asked my spirit guide Francine (whom I'll tell you about later), "Why would anyone have a problem with someone just because they're loved?"

"Many people like you don't understand jealousy, so you can't comprehend it," she replied.

I guess that made it somewhat easier, but I believe that jealousy is one of those emotions that comes in with no rhyme or reason. I plodded onward through this tough time and tried to concentrate on the students I loved so much, but it was a difficult and painful lesson. I did make a strong resolution that whenever I got my own business, I would never let avarice or jealousy abound—and thank God it hasn't.

In every workplace, there's going to be a certain amount of problems with territorialism, but that can be alleviated by teaching everyone to know each other's jobs (where feasible) and to have them float, filling different positions from time to time. This can also help when absenteeism causes problems because more flexibility

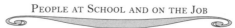

with workers means less loss in production. My own staff members can all pick up the slack for each other.

I also try to tell my employees that I appreciate them, and I'm lucky because even though we have our differences, we have a core of beliefs that holds us together. As the head of various companies and a church, I try (not always successfully) to be as fair and appreciative as I can be. If I'm not there, thank God my people have been with me so long that they understand. They also know that while they're always to be courteous to the public, I've told them that they're never to be defamed, screamed at, or treated rudely. The customer is *not* always right if he or she is being mean and irresponsible. No one accomplishes anything by berating another human being, and no one should diminish another person's dignity. Thank God we almost never get that kind of treatment—I'm convinced that people know where others' intentions and motives lie.

This may surprise you, but as a general rule, I haven't been a proponent of partnerships in business. Sometimes it works out well, but I can tell you that in my experience, more times than not it ends up like a bad marriage, with one party getting the lion's share and the other being left out in the cold. Greed has no place in the working world—or, for that matter, in any partnership anywhere or anytime—but it *does* raise its ugly head. So unless we're driven by a higher purpose, we shouldn't get into business when the temptation is overwhelming.

Finally, I'd just like to remind you that there are always loopholes of opportunity in life if you're not too busy being stressed to see them. I promise you that God will provide. I know this and have seen and proven it over and over in my own life. First figure out what would make

you happy, then put it out there. It will come. And just remember that people like Sister Marcella Marie are dotted throughout our lives as spiritual messengers along the way . . . if we're just open enough to pay attention to them.

♔ ♔ ♔

Chapter Three

FAMILY MEMBERS

*I*n this chapter, as well as those that remain in Part I, I'm going to explore much deeper relationships. These are the ones that really brand our souls and impact our entire lives. This, of course, brings us to our families.

The Parent-Child Connection

They say that we learn about love from our parents. In my case, however, this wasn't entirely true—I was taught about it by my grandmother Ada and my father, but certainly not by my mother. It's true that she grew up in an age when women didn't have much choice except to get married and have a family, and they usually had to go directly from their parents' home to do so. Of course, things in my time weren't that different. In fact, I remember these two girls from my high school who got an apartment together after graduation. They were branded as "love girls," and they never did get married.

My mother was a very unhappy person, and I realized early on that she was also a prescription-drug addict. I think that's why to this day I have trouble with painkillers

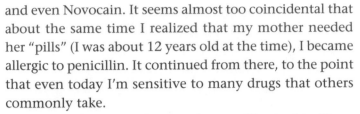

and even Novocain. It seems almost too coincidental that about the same time I realized that my mother needed her "pills" (I was about 12 years old at the time), I became allergic to penicillin. It continued from there, to the point that even today I'm sensitive to many drugs that others commonly take.

I think that we make ourselves predisposed to "family weaknesses" by telling ourselves that we inherited them. Yes, I believe that addictions *are* illnesses, but they can be overcome if we're aware that we picked them as tests for our spiritual growth. It's almost too easy to say, "I come from an alcoholic family; therefore, I'm an alcoholic, too."

Recently, for instance, I met a man in a restaurant who said that his parents were alcoholics, so he was one as well. I said, "No, that's what you *chose* to do. Even more important, if you knew that they were alcoholics, then you could have gotten counseling to help your supposed genetic weakness." Then I went further by telling him, "And since your parents both died of liver failure, that's not a great thing to emulate."

He subsequently tried to use my philosophy against me by retorting, "But I probably picked that, too."

"No," I replied, "you picked it to overcome disease, not to go off track by using it as an excuse to drink."

He sat there quietly for several minutes, and when the waitress came over, he declined another drink. I'm sure that our exchange didn't instantly fix him, but what we *can* do in life is plant seeds—some take root and some don't, but we shouldn't let that stop us from putting them in the ground in a loving and caring way.

My mother was a victim and a martyr, and she used me to keep my father around. I was the apple of his eye, so her favorite theme was this: "Go cheer Daddy up so that he'll be in a good mood." I resented it, but it served me very well in years to come in that I learned to be a performer at a young age.

Mother was never given to affection or words of love—only criticism. I was too tall, my hair was too unruly, and she resented me for making my father happy (even though she was the one who asked me to do so). I knew very early on that I was in a no-win situation with her, so rather than dwell on all the hurt I could have sustained, I shut her out and gravitated toward the warm love of my grandmother, uncle, and father.

Now you can choose to carry around one or both of your parents' mistakes, or you can use them to become a better mother or father yourself. If you don't turn your life's negatives to positives, you spend your days not learning . . . and you end up spiritually bankrupt. Personally, I took what my mother did and how she was and turned it into everything I didn't want to do or be.

In other words, many times we should actually be grateful to such negative entities because they can help us grow spiritually—they strengthen our souls and make us better human beings. Yet too often people use a challenging home life as the excuse to be abusive, or they spend their days feeling martyred. What a royal waste of time! On top of that, everybody gets tired of hearing about how abused they were and how they used this as an emotional crutch year after year. *No one* escapes rejection or pain; it's what we do with it that makes our spirits grow.

Mothers and Daughters

Although the relationship between my mother and me didn't work out, I've seen so many beautiful mom-daughter connections. After losing her mother, one woman even told me, "She was my best friend." Yet some women have never been taught to bond. Men seem to do it with ease, but we women have so many emotions flowing that it's sometimes hard for us to find a common ground. This isn't a criticism; it's merely the way we're made. Girls are close to their mothers when they're young and then transfer their feelings to their fathers (if he's around). This is normal and healthy because it shows that the female is trying to balance herself between the emotional and linear intellect. The mind searches to duplicate itself with a balance of both male and female, and this is especially true with young children.

There's a definite sense of vying for position with the mother that often happens . . . especially during the teenage years. If you can bite the bullet at this time and be a loving friend or spiritual light to your daughter, you'll get through it. You might get a little battered in the process, but you'll be stronger for it. Ladies, as you're reading these words, honestly remember how you were at that age—trust me, it will makes things easier.

Trumpeting that "I was a perfect daughter" won't fly . . . it only demeans your child's soul and estimation. Many times our girls are so much like us that what we see in them is actually a reflection of things we haven't accepted in ourselves. But remember that thanks to our monthly cycles, we gals are more susceptible to emotions. Most of us start very early with intense feelings, diary or poetry writing, and romantic attachments . . .

it's all part of the hormonal flux. Add an environment where this emotional being is neglected or condemned, and you have a full-scale standoff between mother and daughter—and enough bad memories to last a lifetime.

One thing we often do is allow our children to push our buttons—and I hate to say this, but we women are really good at this. I tell mothers to walk away because this occurs in so many relationships, and you can't get anything settled when someone's hormones are racing. Just walk away . . . time will pass, and then you can talk. Overreacting doesn't get anyone anywhere. And remember that "I love you" doesn't count for much if it's not backed by actions. Ignoring your kids or being critical of them isn't loving. Why do you think we have so many gangs? Because young people are looking for a place to belong. We're tribal beings, and the need to belong or be accepted is primordial. Because of our emotional makeup, females seem to really seek approval—especially in adolescence. To be accepted by a mother is the first step in knowing how to bond with other females. "I'm proud of you" is so important, as is "I know you will value yourself as I value you."

Set things up so that your girls can tell you anything without getting yelled at. You may cringe, but muster up your courage to hear what they have to say. Hopefully the introduction of spiritual mores is introduced long before the female reaches puberty. It's not archaic to explain to girls that they're special sacred vessels made by God. They weren't put on Earth just to procreate—they must respect themselves enough to keep their temple from being entered or violated for a mere moment's pleasure. Talk about your life and what you went through or even what a nuisance you were to your parents.

Again, the "perfect" model doesn't fly, especially when dealing with a girl who's fighting with her pain, morals, ethics, and even the times she's living in. Peer groups are tough to stand up to, and sex is everywhere—certainly when it comes to the teenage mind. Not that I want to take on the old puritanical theory of "Cover up!" I mean, *I* wore stretch tops and shorts as a young girl. (Of course we didn't have to worry about all the sexual predators that we do now.)

Keep in mind that negativity *does* beget negativity—no one wants to confide in someone who seems to have her own baggage. Many daughters, unfortunately, become the mother figure to their own moms, causing both parties to lose. So every day when you get up, tell yourself that you have a good life and family; and in addition, you're still young, yet you have enough wisdom to help your daughter.

Sometimes we think that it's dishonest to act positively when we really don't feel it, but how we speak, act, and react causes our mind to follow suit, which is why positive affirmations work so well. Whether you realize it or not, young people are very psychic. So if you're a quiet, constant, spiritual example with the outward appearance that everything can eventually be fixed, your kids will mirror you.

It's important for a mother to be tender, loving, and caring . . . although there will come a time when the growing female isn't so affectionate. However, I sat on my grandmother's lap even when I was 18 because it was a programmed response of acceptance. *Acceptance* is a word that encompasses so much . . . even unconditional love.

I know that we all have a tendency to lie to ourselves, or put off until tomorrow what we might face today. But instead of doing that, be a part of your daughter's life. That doesn't mean that you should drink, smoke, or do drugs with her to show her that you "understand." That's not understanding; that's consent to do wrong. If you put a God-center in your lives, you and your daughter will always have a base to come back to.

Mothers and Sons

Now let's move on to the mother-son relationship. As we'll see with fathers and daughters, this tie can be less stressful thanks to the opposite-sex connection. The relationship between mother and son can certainly be complex, but it's usually not as emotional as that of the two females. You may say that I'm prejudiced because I raised boys, but I also had a foster daughter named Mary who lived with us from the time she was 6 until age 22.

The old saying "A boy is a son until he takes a wife, but a daughter is a daughter all of her life" can be true in many instances, but even in my readings, I find that eight times out of ten, boys stay close to their mothers. This simply proves that women are more resourceful and independent than we give them credit for. Of course I'm not trying to say that we're creating a bunch of mamas' boys, but since men have been tribal from the beginning of time, it's natural for them to try to keep the clan together.

More often than not, if mothers ask their sons, "But if you do it this way, wouldn't you have better results?" it will reap greater rewards than barking, "This is wrong because I say so!" In this way, you're giving them suggestions to see the logic, rather than your being the controlling matriarchal figure. Brutal enforcement never works; it only demeans the individual, especially if he's male. To hit or abuse in any way is never, ever acceptable for anyone; it simply teaches boys that things are acquired through physical violence . . . and the world has had enough of that.

And as I used to tell my high-school girls when I was teaching, males are far more sensitive than we give them credit for. Once upon a time they could be warriors, hunters, and builders; today, most men can't. Their primordial instincts have been squelched by modern-day office structures, and their egos have become quite fragile in the process.

Mothers also can't treat their boys like alien beings or blame whatever negative relationships they've had with males on them. Rather, note that there can be a real camaraderie with sons . . . a true and caring friendship. I'm sure that it was tough for my boys in the early days to have a psychic mother on television. They got a lot of teasing at school, more than they realized that I knew.

The mother-son relationship can be very close and rewarding, especially if your boys can tell you any- and everything. Even if you don't necessarily want to hear it, it's better that they come to you instead of going up to someone on the street. So moms, let your males come to you with their problems with females, smoking, drugs, bullies, sex, and the like; and when they're younger, don't be afraid to step in and try to correct a bad situation. Trying to turn little boys into men is insane—telling them not to cry or to "be a big man" is stopping the emotional side that's so important in their development.

Remember, you can be a spiritual mentor without preaching, and you can be a friend without losing control. The door must stay open so that if a wrong is done, you'll pull your son back with unconditional love and spirituality to the person he needs to be and one that you can be proud of. Do you ever stop worrying? Of course not! But at least instead of feeling guilty, you can say that you did the best you could, and you did it with a God-consciousness.

Fathers and Daughters

Again, thanks to the opposite-sex relationship, the connection between a father and daughter generally isn't a complex one. The father usually loves his little girl because of the male protective factor, and she has an emotional tie with him that sets the tempo for what she'll look for in a mate when she gets older. If he's unfeeling or uncaring, she can very well pick the wrong person in her search for acceptance. (This can work for males, too—if their mother has less-than-desirable morals, they'll most likely look at all women as being no good or to be used and walked on.) So a father should never be above reading a story or getting on the floor and playing with his kids. Even board games can teach a child not to cheat, to lose graciously, or to be clever enough to win.

Yet it seems a lot of people don't display as much affection as they used to. My dad and I kissed and hugged until the day he died. Sure, we hear so much about incest that we're afraid to approach anyone anymore—even our own kids—for fear that it will be misconstrued. This is so wrong, as we've turned into a society that doesn't touch, kiss, or hug; and we're now confined within our own shell of self.

Sometimes the daughter feels that she can't always come to her father about sex or "female stuff" because it seems too personal or even embarrassing. Again, if the lines of communication are open, acceptance will follow. I remember when I had my first menstrual period, my dad came over, hugged me, and said, "Now you're a real young woman." I was so proud, rather than being secretive or feeling ashamed about it.

Because I was open with my own boys, I see my youngest son, Chris, being very forthright and understanding with his daughter. Angelia is in that prepubescent stage, and Chris gives her the leeway to be emotional, as my father did with me. So just like a mother, fathers can be great spiritual, moral, and ethical role models. In the long run, working hard, being fair, and setting a good example isn't as difficult as being subversive, selfish, and uncaring. There's *nothing* weak about a father being kind, gentle, and caring—that's not diminishing manliness. I saw my father cry at sad songs and movies or when I did something that he was proud of. Never once did his emotional outpourings lessen him in my eyes; in fact, they made him seem stronger and even more admirable.

Fathers and Sons

The relationship between a son and father can definitely be complex, since it's the catalyst for the young male's ego to start pawing the ground for its own territory. It's been that way from the beginning of time, but I don't think it has to be. If the two males are treated with respect, love, and honor from birth, then they don't need to exert their muscle. If a father wrestles or goes out and plays baseball with his son, it shouldn't be competition, but fair play. This doesn't mean that you have to let your boys win, but it's important to instill a sense of good sportsmanship. If a young male wants to challenge his father, then long before that happens, the father has set this up by implying, "I'm better than you are."

While boys learn about feelings from their mothers, they also learn this from their fathers by seeing that being emotional, caring, and giving are *not* unmanly ways to express oneself. In fact, a true man doesn't have to constantly exert his macho image. (A male also learns how to trust females from his father.)

If you feel that you have an absentee father, remember that you only need one person who unconditionally loves you to make life shine. You can go through your whole life wishing that you had a particular type of dad, yet there are so many individuals waiting in the wings (other family members, teachers, parents of your friends, mentors, and so on) who can be surrogates, thus making up the full richness and spiritual meaning of your life. If you only concentrate on what you don't have, you're likely to end up with nothing but a festering resentment. So be grateful for whatever father you have, for he's here to make you the best person you can be . . . you just have to see it that way.

Nonbiological Children

We've talked about biological children in this chapter, but what about stepchildren, foster kids, or those we've adopted? Well, no matter how they entered our lives, these boys and girls should take the same place in our hearts as if we'd birthed them ourselves. So many times a stepparent only views the child as his or her spouse's, and this is so wrong. (I've even seen biological parents do this when children misbehave by saying, "Oh, you're just like your father [or mother].") These individuals aren't taking into consideration that yes, there are environmental causes and some genetics involved, but each person should be treated as a soul unto his- or herself. All souls should be treated with love and respect until they prove beyond a shadow of a doubt that they don't deserve it.

As I mentioned previously, I had a foster daughter whom I raised with my biological sons, and I still love her as if she were my own. In fact, I always said that I had three kids. In addition, I practically brought up six other boys—Chris, my youngest son, would bring these kids home to stay "just for two weeks," and they'd finally leave several months later. These are all jewels God gave me to care for, and I treated them as such.

Hate breeds hate, and children will feel it. *Any* child in your charge should be respected and loved, rather than viewed as a burden you've been victimized to bear. No child deserves to be punished for "the sins of the father."

Some Advice for All Parents

The first thing I'd like to remind my fellow parents of is that we can't blame our children for our problems— whether we're tired, going through grief, or in the middle of a divorce, they're still our priority. Oftentimes it's as if the stress of life boils over and then some unsuspecting individual gets the wrath that's meant for who or what is really bothering the person. We see this in homes where the parents have a fight and then the kids get yelled at. If this happens, the adults should simply apologize by saying, "I'm just upset over something, and I took it out on you. I'm sorry." Children will understand this and realize that no one's too perfect to make a mistake.

Yet our children should also be made to understand that we're not "yes" people. In other words, we won't condone every behavior, but we will tell them the truth and love them anyway. As corny as it sounds, appreciation and love conquer so much, while criticism and sarcasm will get us nowhere. I've seen statements like "You're too smart, sweet, and attractive to say those things" neutralize anger. A kind word turns wrath to logic.

If we're nagging and using that old proverbial "Well, in my day, blah, blah, blah," we've lost the battle and the war is on. No one can talk to anyone who's condemning and critical, so rebellion is sure to follow. "I'm there for you no matter what" is a better spiritual adage. I felt that my father and grandmother loved me so much that hurting them would have almost killed me. Unconditional love is a powerful tool—yet it can't be faked because kids will know it.

From raising my own children and teaching at an all-girls high school, I'm convinced that it's better if you let your sons and daughters come to you. I don't mean that you shouldn't keep a tight rein on curfews and friends or discuss alcohol, smoking, sex, and drugs, but their taking the initiative forms a bond. Yet never disclose information given to you in confidence because then the trust is lost. I always left my door open, and sometimes I got too much information, but I'd tell myself that it was better than getting none at all. When your kids can come to you and you're not too busy or harassed, you become their confidant, rather than having them go up to some stranger who could pull them off track. Make the time to speak with them, and if they want to talk, drop everything . . . it just may be so important that it can greatly impact their life as well as yours.

In all relationships with children, we parents should teach spirituality, mores, and ethics. We have to impress upon them that there are spiritual consequences for all actions. This isn't our rule, but God's—the karmic universe will have its way with us, and what we put out with a malicious motive will come back. I instilled that in my children from the beginning. It might not mean much when they're young, but as my grandmother used to say, it will come back to roost in their minds as they get older.

Many times, talking about spiritual issues such as angels, ghosts, spirit guides, and passed-on loved ones seems to be very fascinating to teenagers and can help you form a bond with them (if you can do it without preaching). I think it's because their hormones are urging them to explore the unknown—my grandchildren are very interested in ghosts and angels, for instance, and two of them are pubescent.

Amazingly, I get so many e-mails from teenagers, and at my lectures and book signings, I've noticed that there have been more and more young people in attendance. It's almost as if they're looking for an anchor in this life, which seems to be so much more in chaos than the one many of us grew up in. It's gotten especially hectic in the last 15 years, to the point that the last 5 have been spent in a void of unrest. Every relationship needs to explore the questions "Why am I here?" and "What am I doing?"—the earlier we start this, the easier it gets.

These days there's usually one parent who's dominant, often thanks to a broken home or either a mother or father who works all the time, leaving the raising to one primary caregiver. It's difficult, but if a child has even one strong parental figure who will maintain a tight rein on behavior and keep the lines of communication open, it will work out. I really didn't have a father figure for my children, but my own dad was a strong influence on them. So if you're a single parent, enlist the support of a person of the opposite sex who can at least serve as a good male or female influence to balance out the family dynamic.

Finally, the one thing that parents should never do is try to live their dreams through their children. We hear of the sports-nut dad who couldn't make it professionally himself, so he pushes his son beyond what he can do just to fulfill his own dream; or of the mom who wanted to be an actress or model becoming the overbearing stage mother. Such behavior makes children pawns and takes their lives away. Follow your kids' lead—if they want to be a musician or a stay-at-home mom, then stand and cheer. You can guide but never control, as this brings about resentment and a loss of identity. Let your children be, and don't interfere with their charts.

Children and Their Grandparents

Anyone who's a grandparent will tell you that there isn't anything like it. I have three grandchildren, and I'm really fortunate to be able to live near them and see them often. Although some individuals hardly ever get to see their grandchildren, there's such a feeling of God's

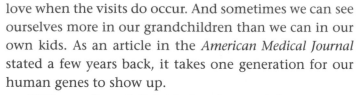

love when the visits do occur. And sometimes we can see ourselves more in our grandchildren than we can in our own kids. As an article in the *American Medical Journal* stated a few years back, it takes one generation for our human genes to show up.

With our (hopefully) tried-and-true wisdom, we can also help our young charges realize that what's important is who they are on the inside, not the labels or expectations others give them. I've never told my grandkids, "When I was your age . . . ," but I *have* found that when they ask me about my early life, things are pretty much the same. Growing up, I had similar problems to those that young people face today—sure, the cars, economy, and styles have changed, but the basic problems are still there. The popular girl, the bully, the favorite teacher, the crushes . . . they're all the same and always will be.

I loved to hear about my own grandmother's life— knowing that what she went through made her strong and spiritual in God's light and gave *me* strength and fortitude. So aside from baking, doing crafts, shopping, or having dinner with your grandkids, tell them stories that have meaning, morals, and spirituality. My grandchildren love knowing about angels and guides, and they like to be reassured that life goes on and that there's a good lesson that can be learned from every incident.

For example, the other night my grandson Willy was talking about his recently deceased dog, Buddy. He said, "We're sad, but Buddy's happy because he's in heaven with God." All three of my grandkids have heard my lectures, and even if they don't believe in what I do when they grow up, at least they'll always carry the knowledge that God loves them. Children used to learn from their parents, but we've lost that in this busy society. So as a grandparent, nothing is more important than giving your grandkids a foundation that they can rely on. By doing so, you'll revel in their discovery of life, the love they give to you, and the euphoria you get from cherishing them. Let them see you be kind and righteous, and don't spoil them to the point that they become jaded.

I think it's wonderful that many of the world's cultures keep the family intact by caring for both their elderly and their young. In the Masai culture of Kenya, for instance, parents live with their grown children and work alongside them and tend to the children of *their* children. I'm not recommending that we all live in the same hut together, but I think that denying kids the benefit of past generations is very sad. To have a family unit that includes grandparents, cousins, aunts, and uncles makes for a richness that we're sadly missing in this society. Such cohesion is the flavoring in the rich soup of our lives.

Siblings

Many times, the duty of the older sibling falls heavily on his or her shoulders. The younger one can be jealous, but also wants to emulate what the older sibling does. You may say, "It isn't fair that I was given this responsibility," but my response would be, "Well, you chose it, so do the best you can with it."

If there's any significant age difference at all, it's natural for siblings to experience some rivalry. The first child has been the "king of the hill," and then all of a sudden this little stranger comes in and takes away the attention. While this situation can breed resentment and jealousy, how parents handle it will alleviate the problem

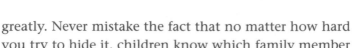

greatly. Never mistake the fact that no matter how hard you try to hide it, children know which family member favors whom. In my case, my father favored me, and my mother favored my sister, Sharon.

While there was a bit of rivalry between Sharon (who's six years younger) and myself, thanks to our mother, I ended up becoming my sister's protector. I knew from a very early age that my mother had a horrible darkness around her, so I ran interference for Sharon, as she'll attest to today. Nothing binds human beings of any age together the way adversity does.

Sisters can grow especially close in a loving family that doesn't play favorites. It's not fun to have your sister wear your clothes without asking, mess up your room, or tear your dolls apart, but if you can get past that, you may find yourself with a marvelous female friend who knows you better than anyone else and shares a history of your life that no one else does.

⊸◈⊷

The brother-brother relationship can be a little trickier because you're dealing with the male ego, which instinctually wants to "rule the roost."

My oldest son, Paul, kept very much to himself and held his worries inside. I tried to crack that shell, but ultimately realized that that was the way he dealt with life. My youngest son is more open, and whatever's bothering him will be right out there (and usually fodder for my ears). Early on, my boys had some rivalry, but thank God they grew out of that. Nevertheless, it wasn't easy raising two sons who were 6'6" and *all* boy. They definitely were their own people and were never close enough to adopt each other's traits, although as they get older I see so many similarities between them. I do think it makes a difference that six years separate them, but as time goes on, the personality gap narrows.

The one thing I thank God for every night is that they're both very spiritual. They're also honest and hardworking and believe in commitment, loyalty, and gratitude. Yes, they have their faults, as we all do. They're quick to anger but also quick to forget (I wonder who they got that from?). They can be stubborn and yet surprisingly giving. Like me, Paul is more spontaneous, while Chris is slower to cogitate and then come to a conclusion. Yet Chris is psychic, while Paul isn't, although he does have a great deal of intuitive ability.

By the way, all children are definitely psychic—we just don't pay enough attention to it or foster their abilities. As I like to say, God gave each and every one of us a "cell phone to call Home," but society, culture, and even some religions beat it out of us. (I've never understood this. If there are prophets in every religion, then why would God suddenly quit making people who could foretell future events?)

⋯⋯

Brothers and sisters can have a very strong bond, as here again we're dealing with an opposite-sex relationship. It doesn't matter who's born first, but the sister often assumes the secondary mother role, while the brother takes on the part of the protector. I've seen this with my own grandchildren in that they can fight, but when one is hurt, the other is inconsolable. When my granddaughter, Angelia, had a dog bite her lip, hospital personnel thought they were going to have to sedate her younger brother, Willy. He was screaming in the emergency room, "Someone help my sister!"

Love conquers all with siblings. Yes, they can fight like cats and dogs, but let one get hurt and the other will either be right there to help or will go to pieces out of sympathy. It's true that adversity brings love to the foreground, but it's a shame that it doesn't tend to stay. If people can just remember what it felt like to know that their sibling was in trouble and carry that over to everyday life, the relationships will be incredibly strong.

Extended Family Members

Aunts, uncles, and cousins make up your extended family. They can be part of your culture, upbringing, and history—both genetics-wise and by contributing to your heritage. Our family is small, so my sons only have two male cousins. Angelia and Willy, on the other hand, have many cousins because their mother, Gina, has a big family and lots of siblings. Paul's son, Jeffrey, only has two cousins, but I love the fact that all of my grandchildren enjoy the richness of family. It gives them a sense of continuance, structure, and even security.

If you're lucky enough to have an extended family, when tragedy hits, you can band together like they used to in tribal times to help each other through your hours of need. This is one of the greatest blessings life can bring to us. I remember one occasion when my whole family went to Cabo San Lucas on vacation. There was a hurricane coming, so we were all sequestered in our rooms with the windows taped up. We couldn't go out, but we played games, videotaped the grandkids interacting, and talked and laughed. We all discussed everything, with the children joining in, and we felt that we were a part of something that might be dangerous (the hurricane) but exciting. The storm never hit hard, but we look back on that day as a highlight of our trip.

Enjoy the good times—listen to, be there for, and care for your loved ones—and if there's too much work to be done, let it go. Your chores can always wait, but the time you miss won't. It goes into a hole, and you can never get it back.

Of course, sometimes things just don't work out with your family members. There can be plain old "bad seeds"—but no matter whether they're parents, children, siblings, or cousins, you just have to bless them and walk away. This isn't wrong; you simply give the situation to God and go away for your own survival, as well as to negate their influence on others you love.

No one wants to subject their children to relatives who are drug addicts, liars, cheaters, or the like—family or not, they don't belong in the circle that you're trying to protect and make a safe spiritual haven. For example, I never allowed my children to be around my mother unless my father or I was present, too, because I didn't want her to heap the same abuse on them that she did on my sister and me. So you have to protect your loved ones, even from your so-called blood relatives sometimes. Remember, though, that instead of carrying this with you as a badge of sorrow, you must use the experience to better yourself and be more effective in keeping your loved ones from physical harm and mental duress.

For your own spiritual growth, leave these people be, and find your own oasis of friends who make up just as valid a family unit as blood relatives do. And in the process, keep in mind all the learning, patience, and tolerance you gained getting there. It's not by coincidence that relationships are often thrown at you like a big vat of stew—each ingredient serves to teach you about compassion and even survival.

♛ ♛ ♛

Chapter Four

ROMANTIC PARTNERS

*I*n my five-plus decades of talking to people, I've found that some common traits run through all relationships. By no means have I ever been, or touted myself to be, above professional psychotherapists (although I do get a tremendous amount of referrals from them); rather, I like to feel that I'm more of a handmaiden to society. What I do know—and you'll hear me constantly hammering this point home—is that if spirituality isn't in your life, then every single one of your relationships is doomed.

You see, we all need meaning in life. Many of us try identifying ourselves by the amount of money, possessions, business success, or power we have, and ultimately find that it leaves us empty. The simple formula is to live for God and our fellow humans in this journey of life. By doing so, we'll become carriers of light and hope in this world . . . and therein lies the true achievement of love in all aspects.

As far as romantic partnerships go, I've noticed that the ones that do make it have what I call "the pyramid effect." In other words, the two people involved adore one another, but they also love God and hold a strong belief in their religion or spiritual growth. These relationships have to be a three-way street or they just won't work.

True Love

Literature is full of all types of lovers, such as Dante and Beatrice, Abelard and Heloise, and Romeo and Juliet. Poetry also illustrates many instances of passion and lost love. For example, there's Alfred Noyes's poem "The Highwayman," in which the protagonist steals from the coaches that travel the roads; and his love, Bess, gives up her life to warn him. And, of course, one of the most beautiful verses of all time comes from Elizabeth Barrett Browning's *Sonnets from the Portuguese:* "How do I love thee? Let me count the ways." Yet in real life she and her husband, Robert Browning, didn't have the ideal relationship, for she was frail and he had a wandering eye.

Now the last thing I want to convey here is that I'm cynical, but there's a big difference between the unrealistic romances of the printed page and what we face in our own lives. Yes, I've had my breath taken away and heard the bells and whistles of passion, but after all that died down, it couldn't hold a candle to how it felt when I cradled my sons and grandchildren, snuggled with my animals, and hugged my friends.

When I was going through my last divorce, I was sitting in my room crying when my granddaughter walked in. I tried to recover quickly, but Angelia was so smart that she ran over, threw her arms around me, and said, "I love you, Bagdah [her nickname for me]." I thought, *What beats this?* It immediately reminded me that true love is pure and spiritual.

Love should be an entity unto itself and unconditional, yet it seems that we human beings have put rules
and regulations on everything: "If you do this, I'll love
you . . . but if you don't, I won't!" That's not love—it's
control and manipulation, and those we supposedly care
for will feel restrained and confined. As I once told the
audience on *Montel,* "Relationships in any form shouldn't
be hard. If they are, something's wrong."

We also have a tendency to want what we don't have,
and even when we do get what we want, we often sabotage it. The simple reason why we can't be entirely happy
is because we don't know ourselves or what we're actually
searching for. All our doubts, worries, and inhibitions can
keep us from loving another and being part of that person's
life. To truly be ourselves requires breaking through the
limitations we've imposed (or let others impose) upon us.
And if we then focus our energy outward, we'll find love.

Since love is God's force, it should be an emanation
of Him in all encounters. You see, no love is ever lost
if you put it out there unconditionally, for someone or
something can use it and bask in its glory. Although you
may never see its effects, that energy will then find a
way of coming back to you—like superglue, some of the
love you've given out sticks to your target *and* your soul
forever.

You can test this for yourself, especially if you're shy.
(Many people would never guess that I'm shy in crowds
because I learned this trick very early on in my life.) What
you can do is deliberately choose a place or party where
you don't know everyone. Sit anywhere, even in a cor-
ner, and pick out one person at a time. "Beam" your love
outward by thinking *I love you,* and really mean it because
that individual is a part of God. Before long, people will

almost miraculously start migrating toward you. Now don't get me wrong—there are some you won't want to attract, but on the whole, love will bring you goodness because it *is* good.

Similarly, if you're frantic to have a relationship with someone, whether it's with a member of the opposite sex or just a friend, your electrical emanation or "aura" will let out a needy cry. This is then felt by all the souls you come in contact with, and they'll back off or leave. We've all been around people like this, and we can instantly recall how repulsed or drained we were by such behavior.

Let me give you an example of what I mean. Friday used to be girls' night out in Kansas City (and I imagine it still is in many places), and five or six of us would pile into my car and go to a local dance or party. One fixture was my friend Sue, and every time we went out, she'd start with, "I hope I meet *him* tonight." We all knew what that meant—her "one and only." In what was the worst type of irony, not only did she *not* meet anyone, but no one ever even asked her to dance! She was a very attractive girl, but her aura screamed out, "Will someone in here love me and marry me?!"

A male friend of mine usually wound up meeting us at the dances, and I once asked him why he thought no one wanted to dance with Sue. He just shrugged and flatly said, "She makes me nervous. I feel like she wants something from me that I can't give her." I tried to talk to Sue about this, but to no avail. She eventually found a browbeaten mama's boy, and they've been unhappily married for more than 40 years now. Of course she doesn't see that she got what she wanted or needed. She's a good person, but thanks to her own lack of soul's worth, she's unfortunately "taken her wares to a poor market" (as my grandmother used to say).

Learning from the Bumps in Love's Road

It's not cynical to say that the only constant in life is spirituality and God, for human beings can really disappoint you. Nevertheless, some people have stayed married for 70 years, and some have friendships that last a lifetime. *My* marriages didn't last, but my friendships have. In all of life there are trade-offs; it's how we handle them that's important.

You may find that what I'm about to say sounds depressing, but stay with me and see if it doesn't resonate with your soul. Life is basically an arduous trip that you endure alone, and the result of that suffering is what makes you grow. You end up learning the true meaning of what existence is about, and you find out how important your relationships with yourself and God are. Yes it's hard, but if you try to maintain joy in your heart, at least you'll have the satisfaction of knowing that you're completing lessons to make your soul grow.

If you have love, compassion, and caring, you'll absolutely enjoy relationships that make you *and* others happy. For example, when I was teaching with the nuns, I noticed that while they did live lives of what others saw as confinement, they also made lifelong friendships with each other and had such an inner peace. (I myself made a lifelong friend in Sister Williams, who's still living in Kansas City and comes to my lectures when I'm in town.) The priests had much more freedom—I'm not going to get into the glaring headlines of what some clergy members have done because the ones I knew were wonderful and compassionate people.

Remember that what we perceive isn't always the

truth. Take celebrities, for instance. While most of you probably feel that they lead pain-free and glamorous lives, I'm here to tell you firsthand (without mentioning any names, of course) that they're often very unhappy with what is supposedly "everything anyone could want." They have problems just like you do.

Who you are inside and what your ultimate goals are will set your soul free. What you think and feel about yourself becomes truth, and others will notice that there's an innate goodness in your soul. If you show joy and a zest for life, people will want to be with you because their inner soul's eye will recognize your truth and emanation of compassion. The bottom line is to ask yourself this: Are you the type of person others want to be around—or, even more important, are you someone *you'd* want to be around? *Relationship* means not lying to yourself or others, and not being determined by what others feel about you. If you're kind and considerate, you'll have great relationships with everyone you encounter.

However, you also need to be selective, because there are few things worse than trying to change or convert someone. If you and your partner can't accept each other, then you've hit a brick wall, and it's time to bless him or her and walk away. Love lost is usually never regained—if it was even really there in the first place.

As they say, hindsight is 20/20; I even find myself looking back on failed relationships from time to time, realizing that I didn't see the writing on the wall, which was practically spray-painted on with indelible ink. Of course, telling yourself how stupid you were doesn't get you anywhere, so don't fall into that trap. If you're a trusting person who doesn't get jealous, have a wandering eye, or think about taking what's not yours, then why would you imagine that someone else wouldn't be the same way?

For example, it wasn't until after the divorce that I started hearing stories about my last husband that truly horrified me. He had alienated so many people by being cruel to them, and he always presented himself as if he were speaking for me. After he left, my loved ones and I were stunned when we began to compare notes about his deceptive acts. He couldn't abide my involvement with my work and family, but so be it . . . I went on and lived my life. I could have beaten myself up for not seeing this; but as I've said many times, if I were psychic about my own life, it would be perfect, right?

You may wonder, "Sylvia, if you've had such awful relationships, who are you to say what's good or what works?" Well, because I've learned from those negative experiences, it brought me to the realization of what's meaningful and important in our connections. As I once asked my spirit guide Francine, "Why have I had to go through so much of life's hell?"

She responded, "If you didn't, how would you know how to empathize with others or help them?"

I replied, "Maybe I could have just read about these things," but she assured me, "No—you had to experience them."

I don't think that someone who's had a "perfect" life could ever understand when others are having tough times. You have to know what it's like in that pit to feel their pain . . . and rest assured that I know what it's like down in that pit.

When they're in a rough situation, people often tell themselves, "But if I don't stay with this person, maybe I'll never have anyone." I say that it's better to be alone than in an abusive, hateful, or demeaning relationship that places you in a dark hole of despair.

After you've learned a difficult life lesson, time goes on and the grief *does* subside—and it's then that you rediscover joy. I promise you that if you have dignity and love yourself, you'll live to love again. For example, I now have a male partner in my life who's kind and caring, demands nothing from me, and takes joy in my success, whatever that may be. He also knows that my true love affair is with humanity, God, and my friends and family.

Relationship Hurdles

Money can cause more problems in relationships than people realize. Now it's not just "keeping up with the Joneses"—it's keeping up with, and getting ahead of, *everyone.* So many times when people meet you, they immediately want to know what you do for a living, what you make, where you live, and what kind of car you drive. Even in personal ads, nine out of ten women will say that they're looking for a wealthy or "financially stable" male. It's almost as if who you really are as a person is less important than how much money you make. Yet if you're really honest with yourself, you'll finally realize that "things" don't identify you, and they never will. In other words, "Whoever has the most toys wins" had better not be your starting point in looking for a mate, or you're going to be in for a lot of heartache.

Don't get me wrong—I'm convinced that God wants us to be happy and even successful, but I often wonder how many cars we can drive, how many places we can live in, how many jewels or clothes we can wear, and how many fancy dinners we can eat. Enough is enough, for excess is a stressful headache. Strangely enough, the people that I've read for who have a great deal of money aren't that happy. They're afraid that they're going to lose their fortune or that people like them solely for what they have (which is even sadder). Certainly we should strive for success and financial security, but we should always be doing it for ourselves and God.

If you have money, utilize it for what it is—a tool to help yourself and others for the overall good. There's a big difference between living comfortably and being decadent. To spend a million dollars on a solid-gold toilet seat is overindulgence, especially when you think of how many poor children that money could feed. And no matter how wealthy you are, if your soul isn't centered or balanced, then you're going to be miserable. You'll look to drink, drugs, food, sex, work, or other outside pursuits to fill the hole that you need to nourish with your own essence.

I'm not going to get into all of the myriad differences between males and females, but from doing readings all these years, I can't help but form some viewpoints that have invariably been proven to be true. Most women, for instance, can't buy the fact that men are as sensitive as we are (if not more so). Their egos are far more fragile than ours, which is why we get so many men out there trying to compensate with cars, careers, or anything that covers up the fact that they can't go out and hunt.

Even when boys are little, their parents warn, "Don't cry—be a little man." This is changing, but for years little boys were told not to act like babies, while little girls could cry and be cuddled if they were hurt. I've

also found that men initially fall into lust, while women fall in love much faster. This is because we women are allowed to love and show affection openly, even with other women.

In addition, many of us grew up with TV shows such as *The Brady Bunch* or *Leave It to Beaver* feeding us the perfect family life: The wife kept the house immaculate, the husband was always involved in raising the children, and both parents loved each other madly. Even today's sitcoms, which are supposedly more "real," project an unrealistic image where everything is worked out at the end of 30 minutes. Life doesn't always imitate art or vice versa, and we can't pattern our lives after any "pie in the sky" relationship. "Why can't you be more like so-and-so" is such a put-down. We're not anyone but ourselves, and that includes some flaws, so the sensitivity and ego of the male and the deep-seated "Cinderella hope" that seems to lie in the female are all right (unless they're carried beyond all reality).

If we're aware of gender differences, our expectations won't be so high or get dashed because we don't understand each other. *Compromise* is also a wonderful word, and certain phrases can help from both a female and male point of view. Try to remember to say, "I will understand that you're sensitive and honor that by not verbally castrating you," and "I will not put you down as a bad wife or mother, because I know that you're trying your best."

We all make what we feel are poor choices—we simply don't see that what we learned from them actually made them *good* choices. So many times we go back in our minds and fantasize about what it would have been like if we had ended up with Joe or Susan or whomever.

Well, it simply wasn't written in our charts to be that way. I also find it funny how the mind plays a cruel trick on us in that we have a tendency to just remember the good times and forget why old relationships didn't work in the first place. To compare, or to be compared, to a ghostly past is unfair and cruel.

This often happens after a death or divorce—we only seem to remember the good times rather than the disappointments or fights. And then the guilt sets in: *If I had done such and such, he wouldn't have left;* or *If I'd been more this or that, she'd still be here;* or *If I'd been there that day, he never would have died;* or *I never got a chance to say good-bye to her;* and on and on the litany goes. Again I must emphasize that this was all written in your chart to happen exactly like it did. To live in the past is not just depressing, but it's truly a lost cause as well.

It's the same as being married but wishing that you were with someone else. I've seen so many times that the grass is *not* greener on the other side; it's actually burnt. You'd better thoroughly search your soul, as well as your ethics and morals, before you start an affair and leave so many lives in shambles. Some folks like to get romantically involved with married people because they either feel safer or they like the ego challenge—either way, this is dangerous territory spiritually. I'm not saying that being with married individuals is always wrong, but motive is everything. Don't look to someone else's life to make yours better . . . you're the only one who can do that.

There's a lot to be said about the premise that you can never break up a happy marriage. For example, after I was finally able to leave my abusive first husband, Gary, my soon-to-be second husband, Dal, was also separated, and we got married two years later. I'm not saying that Dal and I were so righteous in how we handled things, but both of our situations were over long before we ever got together. Timing, motive, and our own spiritual sense of right and wrong guided us here, and everything turned out okay for all parties involved.

Marriage and Morality

I want to take a moment here to talk about what our modern-day world has done to the sacrament of marriage. As we've become more "civilized," it seems that marriage isn't looked upon with the respect that it garnered in the past. The divorce rate is soaring, and most people don't attach as much stigma to it as they did in earlier years. When I left my first husband, there was such a feeling of failure attached to the end of a marriage. In addition, I was a practicing Catholic at the time, and there had never been a divorce on either side of my family. So I was pinned down by my religious, moral, and ethical beliefs, along with the fear of being the scandal of the community.

People were stunned when they heard that I was getting divorced because I'm very private about my life, and I certainly wanted to keep the mental and physical abuse hidden. In those days, you presented a happy face to the world until you realized that you were living a lie, and staying married no matter what was also the prevailing morality in the era in which I grew up. The independence of women was certainly not encouraged in the Midwest in the late '50s and early '60s.

Even when I returned to Kansas City for my class reunion some years back, would you believe that I was one of only two people—out of *125* students—who'd been divorced? I don't want to be discriminatory about states, but since I travel around and talk on the phone to so many people all over America, I find that the divorce rate is higher in the coastline areas than in the middle parts of the country. Is it because there's more temptation and stress in the coastal areas or larger cities, which leads to dissatisfaction in oneself? So many times out of our own insecurity, we make life more complicated than it needs to be—especially if we start looking around for other people to fill our void.

It's now fairly commonplace to meet individuals who are divorced, and single parents abound. Is this because people in general don't have the time to cultivate a romantic partnership? Are we too busy making a dollar to care and love like we should?

Morality has always been somewhat cyclical. For example, in the 1920s it was party, party, party, in reaction to Prohibition, which had been enacted in 1919. Family values were strong in the 1940s and into the '50s, and then rock 'n' roll came along and everyone thought that it was going to be the downfall of our youth. Although peaceful demonstration for change was the "in" thing for special-interest groups in the '60s, the terms *free love* and *drug culture* also came forth, and again moralists thought that our youth had gone to hell in a handbasket. People tend to forget the good things that came out of these years, such as the civil-rights movement and the eventual cessation of the war in Vietnam.

Then came the era in which our attention shifted from the United States to the world, and people such as Egyptian president Anwar Sadat helped to bring about global change in the 1970s. Although the Cold War had been in place since after World War II, Russia was also

changing and eventually became a democracy in the '90s. At that point, America's focus shifted to the Middle East and Bosnia. These days, conflicts around the globe are escalating, and terrorism is the new reality we all have to deal with.

We're now seeing an upsurge from the moralists led by the Republican Party, and whether that's a good or bad thing really isn't the point, for morality comes and goes just like the seasons. We used to be able to handle everyday problems with more aplomb because they were localized, but with negativity expanding into a worldwide phenomenon, our stress levels have become overwhelming. Since 9/11, they've even increased to the point where *every* one of us is involved, and we're not handling the tension well, especially in personal relationships.

Part of the fault lies in technology, because today we get news instantly—and with full graphic descriptions and pictures. We're starting to become anesthetized to the violence, death, and other horrible atrocities that are taking place in the world. You may wonder where I'm going with this. Well, all this stress, inhumanity, and apathy have affected us to the point that we're more uncaring, unfeeling, and prejudiced than ever before. If we're not cautious, we're going to become like animals fighting each other for the last bone.

This carries over into our personal lives and our relationships. People who wear turbans are looked upon as enemies and attacked for no reason, and we're becoming more suspicious and putting up walls of protection around ourselves, both with strangers *and* loved ones. We're overreacting, just as we did in the past with the internment of Japanese Americans during World War II, the Joseph McCarthy "red scare" that was a response to

Communism, the unjust treatment of Vietnam veterans, and the hate and discrimination allowed before and during the civil-rights movement. Now overreaction is rearing its ugly head again thanks to terrorism.

The world will survive (at least for the next hundred years or so), and so will we as individuals, despite all of the stress and heartache we all experience thanks to our inhumanity toward one another. This survival will largely be due to kindling good relationships with each other, which is what this book is about. Although I seem to be on a soapbox here, everything I'm saying directly relates to how we treat each other, how our values are obtained, and how we love. Without love, there can be no spiritual connections or hope of happiness—either for us as individuals or as a planet. And anytime the mores of society dictate what we do, things can get dangerous.

We have to follow our hearts as well as our charts. Although almost all of us stay on track, we often get bewildered or feel guilt if we follow our gut-level instincts. But these are the remembrance of our charts! Nevertheless, we get confused about what's right because we listen to what society dictates rather than to our God-center.

Let's say that you wrote in your chart that you'd have two kids, but then you're not as thrilled as you thought you'd be, or they don't turn out the way you hoped they would. Well, you've got to understand that spiritually following your chart for God doesn't mean that life will be a rose garden. You completed that part of your chart and did the best you could. So it wasn't great—but hopefully you learned and let it go without guilt. In *all* instances, if you do the best you can, you can just walk away. You've done your job, and now it's up to others to follow their charts.

A Few Words of Advice

I've always believed that honesty is the best policy, but I also remember what Father Nadean told our Christian marriage class when I was in college. He basically said that confession is usually only good for one soul—yours.

In other words, if you're getting married, is it so important to unload all the details of your romantic history to your intended just to assuage your conscience? What went on in your life prior to meeting your future mate is *your* life. In fact, many times, releasing your guilt only hurts the other person and puts suspicion out there that can never be erased. Now if a really dark past can come up and harm the relationship, that's different, but to constantly talk about your prior conquests is cruelty, not honesty. No one wants to feel that they fall short of someone who seems to have been perfect.

Sometimes these so-called truth sessions can be beneficial, but they should always be treated carefully. You first have to question *yourself* to find out whether you're just seeing a reflection. In other words, if you lie, you may think that others do as well. So if you're jealous, what are you hiding or carrying over from a past life that's making you suspicious of your partner, especially if you don't have concrete proof? Just because your special someone looks at another attractive person shouldn't set you off. After all, your partner isn't dead, and we should all appreciate the beauty that's found in another person's body, mind, and soul. On the other hand, no one wants to be reminded of their defects and be told how they don't act or look like so-and-so. This can be put under a big heading of insecurity. If it's from your own mind, get help; if it's coming from others, talk to them about it.

The one thing I continually hear and see in my readings is that people don't know how to vent. *Fighting* is an awful word, while *venting* implies, "I want to get this out so that you'll understand what's wrong and where I'm coming from." If we start bringing up old, hashed-over problems, then we might as well bury our relationships because they're either dead or in the process of being killed off in a slow, painful way. We should talk to each other with firmness and respect . . . when we resort to name-calling and finger-pointing, this demeans our souls and leaves our partners in the almost impossible position of defending themselves.

It goes without saying that physical abuse is never to be tolerated at any time or for any reason, but cruel words can also leave a permanent etching on the soul. Claiming that "I was so mad I didn't realize what I was saying" is a lame excuse. If you're that out of control, then there are usually deeper issues that you haven't expressed, causing your emotions to override your reason.

Once they've been said, words can never be taken back. Of course I've had instances when keeping my true feelings inside almost caused me to bite off my tongue, but I learned something very early from my grandmother. She gave me the analogy of going up in an airplane with a feather pillow, saying, "Cut it open, let all the feathers out the door, and then go pick them up."

I naturally looked at her in surprise and said, "You know that's impossible."

She calmly replied, "So is trying to take back the hateful words you let escape from your mouth."

⋘◈⋙

Too many people get married in the throes of infatuation or the hormonal flush of lust. We should all give ourselves time to know another person—I suggest at least a year or two of going through many of life's twists and turns together. Then we can see people for who they really are, not how they portray themselves to be.

From my readings, I've found that people rush to the altar too fast for fear that they'll never get married. I'm convinced that the reason we feel this way is a carry-over from past lives. In previous centuries, people were expected to get married early, primarily because human life spans weren't very long. Women often died in childbirth, and then there were innumerable plagues and outbreaks of tuberculosis and influenza (which even terrorized the U.S. as late as the 1920s). People were usually lucky to live into their 40s. Dr. Zahi Hawass, Egypt's Secretary General of the Supreme Council of Antiquities, once told me that many of the early Egyptians died in their late teens or early 20s, commonly from abscesses in their teeth.

Well, we should rid ourselves of this old past-life morphic resonance and wait until we find the person who's right for us. (Although I feel that it's really crazy to expect someone perfect when we're certainly not.)

Then when you do find that person, keep in mind that complacency and mediocrity are the killers of any relationship in that they give birth to spiritual discord. When this happens, whether the person realizes it on a conscious level or not, he or she begins to look for something more exciting. Of course you're going to wonder at one time or other what life would be like without your partner, just as you dream of a different job or better-behaved children. This is normal . . . until the dreams begin to dominate your life.

Taking someone else for granted is another killer of a relationship; in fact, taking *anything* for granted is a no-win situation because that's when you start to feel that you're entitled to something. No one is entitled to anything—everything in life is earned, and the word *gratitude* should be on everyone's lips on a daily basis.

The other day, my oldest son, who travels with me, said, "Mom, I so appreciate traveling with you, and I really enjoy our time together." This made my day and maybe the rest of my life. How much does it take to tell someone that you appreciate them? It will go a long way in giving someone happiness and confidence, and it will also give you more incentive to please others.

Many times there can be too much interference from friends and family in a love relationship, and when that happens, you really ought to leave the negative influences behind. This doesn't mean that you should ditch good, supportive people, but rather, those who talk ill of your spouse or partner and try to divide the two of you. I've seen many marriages saved by moving away from in-laws who want to control a couple's life, or removing oneself from single friends who want to pull their old pal back into their world of chasing the opposite sex or partying. These are bad relationships that have a definite effect on the couple, but everything turns out fine when the spouses have enough integrity to negate anyone or anything that threatens their happiness.

Then there are the annoying habits that people seemingly can't stand about each other, which belie a deeper resentment. Most of us tend to pick on our partners' idiosyncrasies rather than let the real dragon loose. Whether it's sexual dysfunction, laziness, or any deeper character flaw that we don't want to face, we may become more irritable or even shrewlike in our behavior. We then either communicate meaningfully or create a bigger problem down the road, as no one wants to live with a haranguing person. There are definite risks to meaningful communication, which is why many of us either delay it or don't even try at all.

If you're unhappy in a relationship but want to save it, you have to bite the bullet and at least attempt to talk, or you'll just continue to live unhappily. In many instances, the main fear of meaningful communication is whether the other person will actually hear what you have to say and understand it enough to want to make the necessary changes to improve the relationship. What's the worst thing that could happen? He or she could get angry and either leave or make you leave, abuse you in some way, or refuse to listen and continue to make your life miserable. In each of these scenarios, either mental or physical discomfort is bound to happen, which is why you've probably been hesitating.

Well, this is a decision that all of us have to make at some point in our lives. We fear the pain that might occur with "meaningful" communication, but we must either try it to make things better in the relationship or let it go—which means that we suffer more unhappiness and tolerate it.

No matter what happened in my first marriage, it was somehow my fault. As if it were yesterday, I remember finally looking at my husband and saying, "You're right—everything *is* my fault. Since it is, I want out to give you peace of mind." He didn't know what to say, but it was true—the time came when I didn't care who was right or wrong because I just couldn't take it anymore. At that point, it was time to move on. No one should put up with alcoholism, physical or emotional abuse, gambling, drugs, or any aberration of behavior. It's socially, spiritually, and morally unacceptable.

There's no doubt that we all have a need to couple, yet it can be fulfilled by any number of relationships. It's like the ancient yin and yang—yin is female and dark, while yang is light and male, and the two make a complete circle. So in essence, whether it's male or female, a friend or family member, we still can have the intellect yang and the emotion yin encompassed in our lives. When the two come together as spouses or romantic partners, there's nothing better. As an aside, you can and should make a list of what you want in a mate, but I've also said you should make a second list of what you expect from yourself. When I hear people ask, "Where's my perfect mate?" I often come back with, "That's all well and good to want that, but are *you* perfect?"

I know that I'll keep enforcing this, but so many times we look for one ultimate relationship that blocks out the rest of the world. When we get too focused on just one person, the rest of our life goes begging, and then we feel alone and abandoned.

I'm convinced that we either yearn for the Other Side (where we do have perfect love), or we're taught to expect a false romantic dream by novels and movies. Well, we didn't incarnate just for that. We came down to be in the state of *giving* love, not always receiving it.

♔ ♔ ♔

Chapter Five

OTHER LOVED ONES . . . ON EARTH AND ON THE OTHER SIDE

*A*side from the supporters who make up the foundation of our earlier years, what about the dear friends whom we meet later on the road of life? Some people have told me that after they got out of school, they found it difficult to make friends. Well, in order to have friends, you have to *be* a friend. Hopefully we never stop connecting with other human beings who enrich our lives.

There are those whom we've shared life with, walking through years of joy and adversity together. For example, I met Mary Margaret Ryan in grade school, and we've been friends for 61 years. Even though I've been in California for more than four decades, Mary Margaret and I have always stayed in contact with each other through cards, phone calls, and visits back and forth. We love to talk over old, sweeter times, in which we were able to walk to museums, put on plays, and even steal kisses in the park with some boys . . . and then run all the way home laughing.

Friends are priceless gifts. Along with Mary Margaret, I still have about ten pals left in Kansas City. Recently I was back there and went to dinner with my old chums

Mag and Joe. We were reminiscing about my grand-mother, uncle, and parents, and Joe told me that he learned everything about business from my father. What price can you put on these validations and memories? After dinner, we stayed up late talking about the nuns who taught us, the relationships we had, and the loved ones who had passed on. That evening I took away such a feeling of history with me, along with a sense of loyalty and commitment.

To be identified by your history and its joys and pains is not being dependent; instead, old friends just enhance who you are and where you've come from. As my friend Paula once told me, "Sylvia, we all feel a part of you when you're on TV and through your writings." I grabbed her beautiful face and said, "Dear Paula . . . and you are my dear." When I left Kansas City, I thought that going to this strange land of California meant the end of real friendships. How wrong I was!

I started to teach at St. Albert the Great in Palo Alto, California, and began to make friends with the nuns and some of the mothers in the PTA. Then I enrolled in night school at the College of Notre Dame (which was connected to the University of San Francisco) to get my master's degree. There I met one of the loves of my life— the brilliant and wonderful professor Robert Williams, who showed me what true friendship meant. Although he was gay, he also taught me that love didn't have to be sexual. He used to call what we shared "the orgasm of the mind," and it was truly that. I so loved having these glorious intellectual lovefests with my dearest friend.

We talked about literature, politics, and religion; along with my psychic ability, which he wouldn't give up on. And once as we were driving, he said, "Sylvia, you've never pushed, or asked me why I walk on the side of the street I do."

I knew what he meant and assured him, "I know, and I don't care. I just love you." He grabbed my hand and kissed my palm . . . no more needed to be said, as so much was already understood.

The times that I spent with Bob were some of the most exciting and stimulating of my life. He had a sense of humor that was beyond compare, and as I've never been short on humor myself, we'd laugh until we both had to make a bathroom run. During this time I also became acquainted with the gay community in San Francisco, which gave me a real insight into kindness and laughter. Bob would take me to all of his haunts and introduce me to his friends. (To Enrique, Joey, David, Dennis, and so many others—thank you for all your love and unconditional friendship!)

I don't want to get up on my soapbox again, but I saw firsthand how these men stuck together, helped each other, and cared for one another when one got ill. This was in the first days of the AIDS outbreak, which at the time was just called "the gay cancer."

Anyway, my friendships are varied and with individuals of different sexes, races, and creeds. We should all be so lucky to have a montage of friends from different backgrounds, colors, and religions, for it will make us richer. We think that time, age, and space separate us, but they don't—we *all* feel love, joy, pain, compassion, and so forth.

Even though I kept telling Bob that I wasn't ready to go public with my abilities, after he died in Australia (after I told him not to go), I started the Nirvana Foundation for Psychic Research. It was one of the most difficult periods of my life, but I really started the organization in memory of him. Yes, I felt that he left me too early, but he gave me a purpose, a direction, and a knowing that love comes in all ways and forms and is as meaningful and euphoric as when it comes in the form of male-female romantic partnerships. Bob boosted me up in so many ways, which inspired me to follow my path of spiritual evolvement.

It's almost too obvious to say that every relationship involves give-and-take, but when it comes to your friends, are you giving more than you're getting? Is it all about them and never about you? If you feel drained, anxious, or irritated when you're around them, then that's your soul telling you to go. If you feel relaxed and that no matter what mood you're in, they'll understand, then you have a true friend. True friends will always accept each other—no one can be "up," funny, or entertaining all the time, so if you feel the pressure to always be that way, then your relationship is a lie.

Yet the worst thing that anyone can do in any relationship is assume a position of entitlement. Ask yourself, "What am I entitled to unless I've earned respect, love, and trust?" Just because you exist doesn't guarantee that you'll be loved or respected. Some of the celebrities I've met seem to feel that because of some overblown reality of themselves, they deserve extra-special treatment. Well, they don't. If you're kind and flexible, you'll find that life gives you perks. You may say, "But I do everything for everyone, and I never get anything back." First of all, who's making you do this? And perhaps you never give others a chance to help you. Either you're a victim and enjoy it deep down (or you'd stop), or you're so insecure that you don't feel as if you deserve anything. Humility has its place, but too much is sickening.

Our charts ensure that we come down to learn; other than that, we should use our time on Earth to do as much good as possible and be a help to others. We must live by the simple rules of kindness, caring, and self-worth, and then we can go Home gracefully. And when we decide to have pity parties about those who have hurt or deceived us, we should immediately think of all the ones who *haven't*.

I was with a so-called friend for 30 years who betrayed me in every way possible, but through it all I counted the blessings of all the wonderful people who surrounded me with their love. These included Pam, who has been with me for three decades and through so many trials; her husband, who remembers when I used to hold meetings in my home; Linda, who's like a kindred soul—she's been with me for 28 years, is my associate, and lives with me . . . what ups and downs we've seen!; my dearest Abass, who used to call me "Queenie" (and sadly died two years ago); and newer friends such as Ron, Reid, Nancy, Wayne, the actor Joel Brooks, and so many more. All of these souls make up the beautiful tapestry of my life. And all of you who read my books, watch me on TV, or attend my lectures have also brought me so much love. Because of all of you, I am able to greatly enjoy my work.

The people I love would fill a million pages. Montel Williams just about heads the list—15 years we've been together, beginning with a promise and a handshake. My admiration for him is boundless because he's an incredibly kind and caring man who does more good than anyone knows. What we've discussed and gone through together make it seem as if we've known each other all of our lives. And my dear Dal, who came back into my life after my horrendous last divorce, has been such a gentle and good companion. Then there's Brian from Dutton; my literary agent, Bonnie; Michael Green; and so many more . . . I don't necessarily talk to these individuals every day, but whenever I see them, we just pick up where we left off.

Instead of focusing on what we've lost, let's concentrate on what we have. For example, I still love and see my wonderful daughters-in-law even though they're not with my sons anymore. They're so precious to me, not only because they gave me grandchildren, but because I love them in their own right and we've shared so much history. Why keep harboring negative or vengeful feelings toward anyone who has brought you peace and harmony? Just because their relationships with their partners didn't work out (which has nothing to do with you) doesn't make them bad people.

And while I have dear supporters going back six decades, I've also made fairly new bonds. I've only known Lindsay Harrison since 1998, for instance, but we often laugh about what lifetime we're on now and how it's impossible that it's been such a short time we've known each other. She's one of those people who, when we met, we both felt, *Oh, there you finally are!* As I said recently to 3,000 people at a lecture in Canada, we're all of one mind—that of our loving God. When we meet someone who reminds us of that, that's what euphoria is.

So many times when I'm doing a reading, people will say, "Sylvia, I'd love it if we could be friends," "You can come and stay with me when you're in my state or country," or "I know you so well that I feel we've had past lives together." Well, I'd love to take all these individuals up on their offers, but I simply don't have the time. However, we *are* friends and have known each other on the Other Side or in a past life. I'm so grateful for—and even humbled by—the love I receive, and I try to give it back in full measure. Loving one another is the motor that makes our bodies and souls run, and it's the motivating factor for why we came here in the first place. If we live in the shell of our own loneliness, we really have no one to blame for our misery but ourselves.

Our Furry Friends

Now what about our blessed pets that many times can take precedence over some of the people we've encountered? I'm convinced that our critter companions are like real guardian angels right here on Earth. I don't know where to begin when it comes to my feelings about animal experimentation except to go on a tirade because I'm so against it. After all, no animals come in with malice unless human beings treat them cruelly; when that happens, they just try to survive by defending themselves.

When I was young, I was only allowed birds (my grandmother had canaries and successfully mated them) and cats, which I dearly loved, but when I left home I got dogs. Since then I've had almost every breed, from German shepherds and Dobermans to sheepdogs and strays from the pound. Now I have a golden retriever, two Yorkshire terriers, a bulldog, a West Highland white terrier, a Shih Tzu, a Lhasa apso, a Labradoodle (a Labrador and poodle mix), and a dachshund, and they all have distinct and loving personalities.

They're such a big part of my life, and when I'm away I miss them so, but my homecoming is always joyous. When I'm tired or don't feel well, they seem to instinctively know it and cuddle around me in a quiet, watchful way. And when I go out in the yard to play with them, it's pure bliss.

I had a friend who had terrible anxiety attacks, and every time she experienced one, she'd go out and hug her animals and the negative feelings would go away. It's also a known fact that taking pets to visit autistic children or the elderly will almost always cause them to break out in a smile, for our furry friends seem to know how to neutralize any negative energy. In addition, the bichon frise and Labradoodle don't have the same type of fur that other dogs do, so those who are allergic can usually tolerate these two breeds.

Animals don't care if you're happy or sad, rich or poor, fat or thin—they love you unconditionally. It seems that they can reach people of any color, creed, sexuality, or what have you. I think that this is one of the reasons why I love Kenya so much. In that country you can witness the elephants' majesty, the giraffes' grace, and the hippos' and water buffaloes' strength. All God's creatures, large and small, play a part in making our lives better and ecologically safe. (I should say "for the time being," since we're quickly making our animals extinct and cutting down our beautiful trees at an alarming rate. It's like God gave us this Eden and we decided to make a commercial dump out of it.)

All of our pets have taught us God's unconditional love, and He has ensured that they're waiting for us on the Other Side. What could be sweeter?

Our Otherworldly Supporters

Our relationships with our spirit guides are very special and like no other. I know this from personal experience, as well as from talking to so many thousands of people who have received reciprocation from their guides. These are the nudging spirits who help us stay on track and give us messages all the time.

My primary spirit guide, Francine, has been with me my entire life. I first "heard" her at the age of seven, and it's amazing how many people at my lectures or public appearances saw and described her long before anything was ever written about her. When I'm in research trances and she comes in, hundreds of people have remarked that as time goes on I take on her features—my eyes slant and darken, the bridge of my nose broadens, and I stop lisping. Of course she uses my body and voice box, but her delivery is decidedly different. Some individuals have also seen my secondary guide, Raheim, who came to me much later in life. I don't have clairaudient communication with him (as I do with Francine), but he does come into my body in trance to provide a lot of historical and theological information.

Your own spirit guide stands patiently beside you along this journey of life. All you have to do to receive help is acknowledge your guide and speak to him or her. After you've asked your guide a question, keep your mind still and take the first answer that comes. I know that this can be hard because you've been taught not to trust your first impression, but nine times out of ten it will be the correct "psychic" answer. Be sure to give your guide thanks and love for being your friend every step of the way . . . including on the Other Side.

The more we talk to our guides and angels, God, and even our passed-over loved ones, the more the veil of disbelief will thin; consequently, our conviction will enable these entities to come in and help us more easily. They help anyway, but that belief makes the lines of communication clearer and more effective. These friends, seen or unseen, are a part of the loves in our lives and are also our protectors.

When I was 26, I was in the intensive care unit (ICU), and the doctors didn't know if I was going to make it. I was lucid enough to remember the ICU door flying open, and my deceased grandmother was suddenly standing beside me, holding my hand and telling me that I'd be all right. You can say that I was under sedation, but I was wide awake. As I mentioned previously, I can't take medication well (and any doctor who's ever treated me will corroborate this), so I was *not* sedated. Grandma Ada was truly there in my time of need.

All the loving souls who have passed to the Other Side are still around us. They communicate with us through our dreams, flashing lights, ringing phones, dropped coins, birds and butterflies, moving objects, and a million other events that we often chalk up to "coincidence." (There are no coincidences in life, as everything is charted.)

Then there are our angels, who are always in quiet attendance but can be very active when needed. There have been countless cases of "strangers" helping people in need, and when the rescued individuals turn around to thank them, the saviors are gone. Well, these are angels who came down in human form for a short time to assist or provide solace. Angels are absolutely the unsung heroes of this life, so give them a nod, a word of love, or appreciation in some form. They don't need it because they do their work happily, but it will make *you* feel better.

❦ ❦ ❦

Chapter Six

OURSELVES

$\mathcal{T}$he next relationship I want to explore, which may seem strange and something that we don't often think about, is the one we have with ourselves.

Are you a friend to *you?* Do you even like yourself? If the answer to these questions is yes, you're in good shape. If you hesitate, don't know, or answer no, then you have to get a handle on the fact that how you connect with yourself spiritually, emotionally, and even physically is vitally important.

We've been taught not to love ourselves because it's supposedly selfish. No, it's not (unless it's at the exclusion of everyone else). We have to love ourselves; in fact, I believe that we never reach our true spiritual growth unless we can take joy in our own company. We need downtime with ourselves more than ever now in a world that's so full of noise and stress.

I have a friend who can't be alone even for a minute, so she continually has people coming and going, phones ringing, and guests staying over all the time. Don't get me wrong—when my boys were growing up, our home was a beehive of activity, but even then I could retreat to my room, read, listen to music, sew, or just be quiet with my thoughts or prayers. Of course I like myself, but getting to that point meant striving to be the person God wants me to be. You see, if you try to do the best you can in this life, emanating love and kindness and never intentionally hurting anyone, then you'll be a person whom you can love and like. And then you'll truly be able to love others, too.

You have to confront the fear of exploring who you are—you can't just hide behind a wall of guilt or feelings of unworthiness or you'll sabotage yourself. The first step is facing your emotional problems. These are usually harmful patterns that you keep repeating, such as the judgment of others or insisting that everyone should do what *you* feel is right. If you're so busy condemning people, you'll never have the time to know, much less love, yourself. So overcoming your destructive patterns can kick-start your growth and self-love.

You also have to face life full on and not shy away from the mountains you have to climb, for each challenge you encounter makes you stronger and more proud of yourself. And in the process, you'll become aware of your strengths, which will lessen your weaknesses.

Speaking of weaknesses, it can be helpful to discover where you come up short. Of course this won't be a pleasant process. After all, questions such as "Am I too self-absorbed or guilt ridden?" or "Am I too much of a perfectionist, not only with myself, but with others as well?" can be uncomfortable, but uncovering their answers will help lift off the heavy layers of behavior that have been keeping your soul from experiencing growth.

In addition, asking yourself what you want from life and what goals you've set for yourself will help you focus. Unless you have an ambition, be it large or small, you're going to feel useless, like a ship without a rudder. If you simply keep your eye on the target you wish to reach, you'll do so.

I know it can be easy to fall into the trap of "I can't do it . . . I'm too weak, afraid, old, young [or whatever your particular excuse is]." Although your chart is set and your soul knows what it needs, many times a negative environment or certain types of programming can cover up who you really are—an entity made by God who is unique and different from any other entity in the universe. Just by knowing that, you can drop those heavy, binding overcoats and set your soul free. But most of all, you have to believe in yourself and trust that even in tough times, your own resources will carry you through.

Now let's get to the relationship we have with our bodies. I like to think of our physical shells as vehicles we inhabit, and if we drive them too hard and never give them the proper gas, oil, fan belts, spark plugs, and the like, they won't last and will fail us.

I also believe that our bodies are our temples, given to us by God. Naturally we shouldn't get too crazy with this. I also believe, as the Greeks did, "Everything in moderation." Any type of fanaticism, whether it has to do with religion, health, or politics, makes me nervous. I believe in eating right, exercising, and not drinking alcohol to excess. (I can't drink at all because I get sick.) I also don't think you should take recreational drugs, eat an abundance of sweets, smoke yourself to death, or take every pill that a doctor will prescribe for you. Sure, you need medication at times, but you must have a real and thoughtful relationship with your body and treat it with respect. If you do, you won't be depressed, tired, or cranky, and your vehicle will drive you around in style for years to come.

The Things Around Us

This may seem inanimate and a bit weird, but everything in life is a type of relationship. Books, for instance, have been a large part of my life. My grandmother only went through the eighth grade in Germany, but her father had a library that filled all four walls of his study. She told me how she started at one end and continued until she'd read every book. She was also the most well-versed person I ever met on the subjects of literature, politics, theology, and social norms; she gave me so much of my love for learning. She used to say that books are our friends . . . and they genuinely are.

Reading not only makes you more knowledgeable, but it also can inspire you in many ways. You may find yourself saying, "Well, if they survived *that,* so can I." I have to admit that I love autobiographies and historical books for that very reason; however, my all-time favorites have always been theological tomes, which I still devour.

The Bible has been interpreted in so many ways—hundreds of monks and theologians have edited it countless times into myriad variations—that you really have to draw your own spiritual and logical conclusions. I recommend that you read the Nag Hammadi texts and the Dead Sea Scrolls, for they haven't been tampered with. And delve into other religions' holy books, such as the Koran or Bhagavad Gita, if for no other reason than to give yourself more knowledge and perspective in coming to your own spiritual conclusions. You have to find what sits right with you—if it doesn't, then just disregard it.

What about other types of communication, such as newspapers, radio, film, and even television? All of these forms of media can enhance our relationship with the world around us and lend themselves to making us better, more informed, and more interesting people. I'm not a snob, but I really prefer to watch something that's informative and challenging to the mind, such as the programming on the Discovery Channel, A&E, the History Channel, and TLC. And when I go to the movies, I tend to enjoy films about historical figures such as Mahatma Gandhi and Elizabeth I (I also dearly loved *Braveheart*), along with comedies and lighthearted fare.

As an aside, I find that everything is so high-tech these days, yet lacking in substance. Even in our movies, we rarely see performances with depth, morality, or meaning—it's all in the "blue screen" special effects. I did enjoy *The Matrix*, but I really didn't understand why they had to add all those technical gyrations to illustrate good and evil. I don't want to sound too stodgy, but Taylor Caldwell's *Dialogue with the Devil* and *The Devil and Daniel Webster* by Steven Vincent Benét are two books that blow away any movie on the subject.

⋘◊⋙

Getting back to material things, I've seen many people who have a *real* relationship with them—their houses, cars, or wardrobes become their be-all and end-all. Well, when *any* thing becomes too important, the soul will go begging.

Everything in life is changing and moving; and jewels, sports cars, and mansions are all just on loan to us if you think about it. No one takes anything with them to the Other Side except what they've done for God, and no one whom I've talked to over there has ever missed their stock portfolios.

This doesn't mean that we have to live in dire poverty, since money allows us to be comfortable and have the freedom to aid others. So many people have asked me, "Do you know how wealthy you'd be if you didn't support so many other people and endeavors?" I'm sorry, but the joy of helping outweighs any material gain I could ever have. I believe that God says, "If you take care of mine, I'll take care of you."

What's important is the small flower garden outside the room in which I do phone readings. The birds that sing, the flowers that bloom, the bed that has the pillows I love, the comfort of a warm blanket on a cold night—all of these are God's blessings, yet so many times we take these items for granted. Gratitude is the sister of love, and if you add those concepts to all the *things* in your life, you'll fulfill your spiritual lessons and stay on track.

Our Rituals

This may seem a little farfetched, but we do have a relationship with our rituals. For example, think about your routine before bedtime: You lay out your clothes, put water on your nightstand, make sure the alarm clock is set, and check that the doors are locked. Or when you get up, you shower, have your coffee, read your paper, and so forth. You probably even have a ritual at the grocery store, including which aisle you'll go down first.

As you can see, our relationships with our rituals do give us a sense of order and security—disrupt them and we can feel off balance. They also have the power to give us a sense of togetherness in a common goal, enrich customs, and bind us together spiritually, especially if they start in the family unit. Rituals are great as long as they're not subversive, controlling, or occult.

Humankind has always had some type of relationship with their gods to ward off evil spirits; consequently, religious ritual can become very severe and even cruel. I've never been a proponent of too many elaborate rites, but I'll defend anyone who wants to participate in them, be it in a church, mosque, temple, or synagogue; kneeling on a prayer cloth or padded knee rest; or chanting or singing.

In the mornings before my readings, I pray that I'm a true channel, and then I surround everyone with the white light of the Holy Spirit—including any negative people I may encounter. (So should you, for it will make your day so much better.) At night I place light columns around the world and ask for angels to attend me, my family and loved ones, and every person on Earth. When we as a group come together in positive rituals, they can give us grace and healing energy and make the world a better place.

Our Special Places

Now let's discuss the connections we have with the places we love. I'm fond of all the countries I've visited, especially Greece, Turkey, and Egypt, but there's something special about Kenya. When I first got off the plane

on my initial visit, I instantly felt that I was home. I loved everything—the shops, the animals, the smell of the markets, and the kind and wonderful people who were always smiling.

There's a pantheistic belief that we're all part of nature and that God is in everything. I believe in part of that—everything may not have a soul like humans and animals do, but everything *is* a mirror of God's love.

For example, I was sitting in the backyard the other night with my granddaughter, and we were listening to the crickets, smelling the pines and the grass, and gazing at the stars. At that moment, we both realized that we all were parts of God's creation. I don't run around hugging every tree, but I feel that our relationship with the beauty of nature around us is God's way of giving us joy. We don't take enough time in our harried society to simply notice the stars, clouds, trees, or hills; and I certainly don't think that it's corny to realize that each tree and blade of grass was put here by God for us to enjoy, love, and cherish.

We really haven't treated this planet very well, but we *can* experience its joy. Whether it's our plants or pets, the smells and flowers of spring, the brisk air of winter, or the crunch of leaves in the fall, these things are all part of the beauty of God's creation. We always say, "Take time to stop and smell the roses," but there are so many other sensory feelings we can experience. Take a few minutes to form a unity with nature, as it truly is an elixir for the soul and will help you strengthen the connection you have with yourself *and* God.

👑 👑 👑

Chapter Seven

GOD

*W*e can read hundreds of books or view countless movies about every single type of human interaction, but they never seem to get to the most important relationship of all: the one we have with God.

From prehistoric times to the present day, there's been an innate force in all human beings that makes them adore, worship, or fear something greater than themselves. I don't care if people say that they're atheists, for there's always something that they revere more than their own selves.

Thanks to the trials and tribulations of our charts, we might feel that God doesn't care about us. This is so untrue—He is always there, holding us firmly in His love. Yet being His children who wrote our own charts, we have to learn our lessons and experience them for our own souls' progression. I always say that God does answer all our prayers; it's just that He sometimes says no.

I live with, and for, God every day and try to teach that to all who will listen. However, I do have a problem with faith. We're always talking about it—faith that a relationship will last, faith in God, or *faith* as a synonym for *hope*—yet there's nothing more intangible. There's a big difference between knowing and just having faith. Faith always carries with it the stress of fear and being wrong; knowing doesn't have that stress, so you're then able to give your all to your own spirituality and helping others.

Faith and hope can breed the fear that you're wrong, and fear can then be used against you, clamping off your spirituality . . . while knowing has the sweet and wonderful sense of security and spirituality that no fear can penetrate. For example, when a preacher or religious figure says to people that they'll go to hell if they don't behave in a certain way, those who only have faith and hope in God will have the fear of going to hell with them throughout their lives. But those who *know* also understand that God is all-loving and merciful and would never condemn anyone to an endless pit of hellfire and damnation.

Faith can only take you so far, for fear rules those who have it and disrupts their spirituality to the point where they become judgmental, condescending, condemning, prejudiced, and totally lacking in tolerance for other beliefs. Their fear leads them to do this, for they're always afraid that they may be wrong in their own belief system. Knowing, on the other hand, eliminates all of this need to be right and lets the soul concentrate on doing good works and loving God instead of fearing Him. If your relationship with God is rooted in logic instead of faith, which can be blind and full of hope, you'll be better equipped to deal with life and all of your relationships.

How we live and come together in spiritual oneness to help others underscores our relationship with God. Keep in mind that while spirituality is truly food for the soul, we sometimes confuse it with religion. Religion is an *expression* of our spirituality, while spirituality itself resides within us and helps guide our actions. The recent inappropriate behavior of some clergy members is a terrible breach of confidence and trust, but it shouldn't affect your true spirituality.

Those who practice the Judaic religion are much to be admired for the fact that their religion is not only part of their holy days, but also a component of their everyday lives. You don't have to agree with their particular beliefs, but the relationship between spirituality, religion, and day-to-day activities should be a template for your own life. In other words, spirituality should be incorporated in your every action, especially in your religion.

Spirituality doesn't always come easily, but once you open up even a crack, God's love will pour in like a deluge of bliss and happiness. If you incorporate God into your life, you'll quickly be able to see how that connection dispels some of the uselessness, depression, and futility you often feel. Whether it's the teachings of Buddha, Mohammed, or Christ—or whatever your belief may be—after a week (or even less) you'll find that you feel better.

I then recommend that you progress to using visualization, such as sending out columns of God's love or placing the white light of the Holy Spirit around you and all those you love. Then go further and ask your angels to attend you and give you protection and love, call on your loved ones who have passed on to the Other Side, or speak to your spirit guide. If you use all the tools that are available to you, they will do wonders.

Finally, please remember that the many facets of God and our relationship with Him are pure and constant. While people can be erratic and given to spitefulness or aberrant behavior, never ascribe these petty actions to God. They are simply not in His nature . . . only ours.

Personally Speaking about Spirituality

One recent evening I happened to catch a news program's profile of an evangelist who made millions off of his followers. While he'd allegedly given quite a bit of money to children and different relief funds, it wasn't much in comparison to the millions he'd taken in. He and his organization purportedly took in an estimated $80 million to $100 million and gave fewer than $500,000 to charities. The investigation said that this man lived a lavish lifestyle thanks to the so-called healings he'd done, yet not one person who'd been "healed" could produce any medical report or physician to substantiate it. And when asked why he wouldn't talk to the news team, the evangelist replied that God had told him not to. How wrong it is to take people's money under the pretense that God talks to you! Maybe God *does* talk to him, but I don't believe that He would say not to speak to reporters.

This is what worries me about greedy occult operations that have been couched in biblical terms to fool people. All money taken under pretenses such as these will only come back to bite the person who took it, for it's truly ill-gotten gain. The relationship with God is pure and not to be paid for. Of course my church and others need money to operate, but to bilk people out of their hard-earned cash is truly evil.

Hypocrisy is rampant in religion and probably always will be because certain religious figures just can't reconcile their human-made dogma with the love and tolerance of God. Well, the key to tolerance is to live and let live, to let those who believe differently than you do have their own beliefs and still love them. This reminds me of a sermon I gave many years ago at Novus Spiritus, in which I related how I had a client (without mentioning any names) who was a wonderful soul, very loving and spiritual. As I looked over the congregation, I found that all were of the same mode—loving and spiritual—but then I decided to test it. So as I was ending my little sermon and gazing at this sea of wonderful faces, I let them know that the client I was talking about was a prostitute . . . and waited to see their reaction.

A wonderful thing happened—there was no adverse reaction from anyone in the congregation! I smiled and thought that our church must be doing a good job, and I took more than a little pride in the work of our ministers. My point here is simple: What people look like, what they do for a living, and what they believe does not necessarily make them bad men or women. Good and spiritual individuals come in all sizes and shapes; from all racial, ethnic, and religious backgrounds; and from all corners of the world. To learn tolerance, *do not judge.* Also, be open to the diversity of humankind, for you'll find that all people are basically the same . . . and most are basically good.

Whenever someone comes to me and asks to become a minister, I stress that this is not a lifestyle that starts when they put on their collars—it's a lifetime commitment that will permeate every facet of their being. They must completely dedicate themselves to helping and ministering to the needs of others, using their spirituality as the driving force in doing work for God. It actually becomes their life, as every day is dedicated to doing for others on behalf of God.

In our church, the ministers are around to talk to people about problems, not just sermonize. We then give a speech about Gnostic philosophy the way Jesus taught it, not the way people have interpreted it. Then we do a closing prayer and the ministers request that anyone who needs help stand up (if they wish) and ask for special prayers. After a final prayer for love and protection, we're done. Ministers are then available for counseling and healing after the service. It's a coming together in a community that believes the same things and follows Christ's teachings as well as other Gnostic writings and guidance. We can't and don't smother our relationship with God in a lot of bells and whistles. I'm always amazed that people don't realize that God always knows our hearts and everything about us.

Yes, I believe in prayer because it brings us grace and keeps God in our hearts, but I'd just like to remind you that when it came to their relationships with God, all of history's spiritual messengers were very simple in prayer—they practiced what they preached by going out and being with the people. Christ never erected a church, and neither did Buddha. We are temples to God, and that's all we need.

Do you realize that we used to learn spirituality at home at our parents' knees? Pre-Christian–era spirituality was practiced in the home, but it was also a community affair. Whether early humans gathered around the shaman, the high priest or priestess, or the wise holy man or woman, it was a bonding of friends, family, and loved ones while also connecting with God.

Then the cold temples went up, all marble and white. The priest or minister was separate and put on a pedestal, both literally and figuratively. The rest of us were relegated to taking a partial role in the ceremonies, and only on cue. The officials dressed differently and supposedly knew more than we did because if a question was

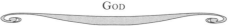

asked, the answer was often, "It's a mystery." This could make us feel that they really *didn't* know anything . . . and why was that? Or that they did know, but we were too stupid to grasp it. The place where we once gathered on equal ground grew into a cold, sometimes forbidding space that led us to start questioning ourselves and each other. Families began to no longer pray or stay together, our roots of belief had been pulled up, and our spirituality (whatever that may be) was now taught by an impersonal priest, minister, rabbi, or other cleric. The result was that we ended up not *at* a knee but *on* our knees.

I always taught my boys spirituality. It didn't matter if they didn't buy dogma; I figured that if they wanted it, they'd find it. They grew up with my philosophy and concepts—the white light of the Holy Spirit, angels and guides, an all-loving God, and so on—and they listened to my lectures from the time they were small. Even though I don't think a lot of it sank in, every so often I'll hear my words come back to me from one of my sons. It's not because they're parrots—trust me, they've always lived their own lives. But like my oldest son, Paul, once said to me, "Mom, I relate to what you taught us because it's logical." And then he continued, "And if it wasn't, I'd just think you were crazy and love you anyway." I just replied, "Thanks, son . . . I think."

When I look over at this tall male with beautiful eyes—who's also my friend and bodyguard; my manager who helps coordinate my events, arrange itineraries, and handle my bookings; and a successful businessman in his own right—I marvel, *How blessed I am!* And then I look at my other strapping son who's also my friend and shares the same work that I do, and I consider myself twice blessed.

Anyway, I've found that those of us who have a strong belief in God have it easier than those of us who don't. God is our basis for being, our solace and comfort through hard times, and He is always there for us no matter what happens.

As those in my church and I firmly believe, helping others is the basis for the greatest spiritual love affair you can ever have, and it doesn't have to come back to you (although it will)—just the act of doing for others will make your heart swell and your soul expand to magnify the Lord. If you even just "white light" each other, bless someone with a "May God be with you," or call on the angels to watch over your significant other, you're bringing in a strong cement to your relationship with God. Far more power than you realize comes along with just a few words or actions.

So why not create a prayer circle just one night a week for your family or loved ones? When you do so (by lighting a candle, burning a petition, and praying to overcome problems and effect healing), you'll come together and create a bond. Let your kids gripe for a while—soon enough you'll be surprised at how young children and even teenagers will verbalize some hurt or wrong that they're experiencing. Maybe they never would have opened up otherwise, but because everyone else in the circle is doing so, they don't feel so foolish; at the same time, you can get great insight into what they're dealing with. It's a win-win situation.

This doesn't have to turn into a four-hour meditation or prayer session—short and sweet is good; long and boring is a punishment. And realize that God *does* know what you need and want, but prayers bind us closer together and elevate us to Him.

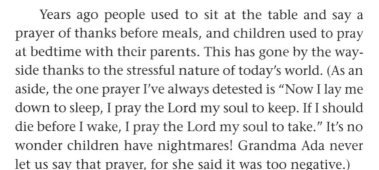

Years ago people used to sit at the table and say a prayer of thanks before meals, and children used to pray at bedtime with their parents. This has gone by the wayside thanks to the stressful nature of today's world. (As an aside, the one prayer I've always detested is "Now I lay me down to sleep, I pray the Lord my soul to keep. If I should die before I wake, I pray the Lord my soul to take." It's no wonder children have nightmares! Grandma Ada never let us say that prayer, for she said it was too negative.)

What happened to just "God bless my family" or a special petition, even if it's as simple as "Help me pass my spelling test tomorrow"? It takes only a few minutes of your time to cement your entire family's connection to God through the common denominator of talking to Him in a family circle or through bedtime prayers. And the seeds you plant early on will have lifelong effects—both of my boys still have their own prayer groups, light candles, and burn petitions.

We're given these spiritual tools to be helping aids along the way, even though our charts are already written, and they help us make the most important relationship we can have even stronger and sweeter.

♔ ♔ ♔

PART II

How Do Our Life Themes Factor In?

Chapter Eight

A BRIEF OVERVIEW
OF THE 47 THEMES

*L*ife themes are the courses of learning that we pick before we come into this existence, sort of like majors and minors in college. I chose to focus upon them in this book because they play such a significant part in determining the success or failure of any relationship.

Sometimes your themes will fit well with those of others, while in other cases they'll greatly conflict. If you're studying to become a doctor, then you need someone who's supportive enough to go along with your goal. A person who thinks only about him- or herself won't understand your need to heal, the time you have to devote to help others, or the demands placed upon you. Consequently, a hole will begin to appear in the fabric of the relationship. This doesn't mean that you can't make it work with someone who challenges you, but either way, the process will help you realize more about yourself and your own chart's lessons.

Although I described life themes in detail in my previous books *Adventures of a Psychic* and *Soul's Perfection* (the second book in my *Journey of the Soul* series), I've never approached them from the relationship aspect. I also felt that it couldn't hurt to revisit each of them here before continuing on.

The 47 Life Themes of Humanity

1. Activator. The focus here is to perform tasks that others have failed to accomplish. These may be truly gargantuan or quite menial, but the focus is always on getting the job done right. Activators, often called activists, are the turnaround artists or troubleshooters of the world—the ones who successfully reverse failure. Naturally, these souls are in great demand and so have a tendency to spread themselves too thin. Activators should make every effort to confine their energies to tasks where a genuine opportunity to achieve beneficial change exists.

2. Aesthetic Pursuits. Music, drama, painting, sculpting, and writing are included in this category. An aesthetic theme is not to be confused with a little "flair" for one of those enterprises; rather, when an aesthetic theme is present, the soul is driven by his or her innate talent. A need to create manifests itself at a young age and dominates the individual's entire life. If the secondary theme is a complementary one, the person will have a long and productive career. If not, any acclaim and privilege he or she receives may lead to tragedy. The agonized existence of Vincent van Gogh reflects a tragic case of a conflicting secondary theme.

3. Analyzer. The rest of us learn from the Analyzers' continuing scrutiny of the most minute details, for they want to know everything about a subject, including how it works and why. Analyzers are afraid that they'll miss something or that some detail will be overlooked, so they thrive in scientific or highly technical settings, where

their skills are vital. In everyday situations, their challenge is to let go and trust the senses. After dissecting the behavior of others, Analyzers should ask the Holy Spirit for enlightenment to transcend the physical evidence.

4. Banner Carrier. The first lieutenant of the Cause Fighter may be found picketing, demonstrating, or lobbying; these souls also fight against injustice. The key to success in perfecting this theme is moderation, tact, and discrimination—it's far better for these individuals to select one cause and see it through than to scatter their impact among many.

5. Builder. Builders are the cornerstones of society, the unsung heroes and heroines of wars, home lives, and organizations. Good parents are often Builders, enabling their children to go on to a much larger canvas. Without these cogs, the wheels of society would never turn, yet Builders rarely receive credit for the accomplishments made possible by their efforts. They need to keep in mind that not all prizes are won on this plane of existence—often those who get the credit on Earth are not actually perfecting as rapidly as Builders, who help to make their accomplishments possible.

6. Caretaker. As their name implies, these souls take care of people, and generally do so with joy. For example, Rosie, our family's maid, looked after the house, walked me to school when I was little, and spent her whole life joyously being a part of our family until she died. She'd been married at one point, but her husband had died in World War II. She then became attached to my grandmother, and thus came to care for our family.

7. Catalyst. Catalysts are the networkers and innovators, those agents of action who make things happen. They're the classroom stars whom everyone aspires to be, the ones invited to parties to ensure that everybody has a good time. Catalysts are essential to society for their innovations (Ralph Nader is a prime example), generally have boundless energy, and actually appear to thrive on stress. They must have an arena in which to perform, however, or they become morose and counterproductive.

8. Cause Fighter. The number of crusades is infinite—peace, whales, hunger, and so on—and the Cause Fighter will either be drawn to them or will create more. These souls fulfill an important function by speaking on behalf of others who are perhaps too absorbed with their own themes to address social issues. Cause Fighters have a tendency toward impulsiveness that can place them and others in jeopardy, so it's essential that they consider the possibility that the cause itself may be minimal compared to their ego involvement.

9. Controller. The challenge for this individual is obvious; in fact, Napoleon and Hitler were typical examples of this theme manifested in its most negative sense. Controllers feel compelled to not only run the broad overall show, but to dictate to others how they must perform the smallest details of their lives. In order to perfect, these individuals must learn self-control and restraint.

10. Emotionality. Both euphoric highs and devastating lows—and every subtle nuance of emotion in between—will be felt by people in this category. Emotionality is frequently a secondary theme of poets and artists,

and it will indeed enhance creativity while imposing a severe challenge. The recognition of a need for balance is vital here, as is the establishment of intellectual self-control.

11. Experiencer. It's not unusual for an Experiencer to go from flower child to bank president to vagabond touring the world in a self-made boat. Experiencers dabble in nearly everything and master many of their pursuits, and wealth is merely a by-product of their multifaceted endeavors (Howard Hughes is a well-known example). Good health is essential to Experiencers, so it's important that they don't jeopardize it with excesses.

12. Fallibility. People with this theme appear to always be at the wrong place at the wrong time, for they've entered life with a physical, mental, or emotional handicap. Helen Keller, who as an infant contracted a fever that left her deaf and blind, is an excellent example—her triumph over these so-called hindrances is an inspiration to everyone. It's important for those with a Fallibility theme to remember that they chose this path in order to set an example for the rest of us.

13. Follower. Initially, Followers might have preferred to be Leaders, but on some level they decided not to make the necessary commitment. The challenge for Followers is to realize that leadership is impossible without them and thus recognize their own importance. Perfection comes from accepting their self-chosen theme and providing the Leader with the best support possible. Yet discrimination is also necessary here in deciding exactly who and what to follow.

14. Harmony. Balance remains vitally important to those with this theme, and they'll go to any length to maintain it. Their personal sacrifices are admirable up to a point, but the real challenge lies in the acceptance of life's wrinkles. Remember that what can't be changed must be adapted to and accepted.

15. Healer. Healers are naturally drawn to some aspect of the helping professions, be it physical or mental. The good they do is obvious, and the only danger is that they can easily become too empathetic. It's imperative that those with a Healer theme pace themselves so that they avoid burnout.

16. Humanitarian. While Cause Fighters and Banner Carriers cry out against the wrongs committed against humankind, the Humanitarian theme takes these people into the action itself. Humanitarians are too busy bandaging, teaching, holding, and saving to have time for protests. Those in this category aren't all that concerned with the concept of evil, and they're inclined to excuse humankind for its faults. Since Humanitarians don't just help out family and friends, reaching far beyond to any- and everyone who touches them, they're in danger of overextending themselves. The challenge for the Humanitarian—*my* challenge, in fact—is to avoid physical burnout through self-love and nourishment.

17. Infallibility. Those in this category are born rich, attractive, witty, and so forth. Yet when we consider that perfection is everyone's universal goal, we find that this theme is actually one of the most challenging. There's often a tendency toward excesses of all kinds here, almost

as if the individual wants to tempt fate. Curiously, there may often be a lack of self-esteem that causes those with the Infallibility theme to fear that he or she isn't lovable as an individual. The goal here is to truly accept the theme and learn to live with it.

18. Intellectuality. Here is the theme of the professional student. Charles Darwin, who used the knowledge that he acquired through intensive study to experiment, hypothesize, and eventually publish, is an excellent example of one who's perfected this theme. But since knowledge for its own sake is frequently the goal among intellectuals, there's often a danger that the information they've so ardently sought and painfully acquired will go nowhere.

19. Irritant. Deliberate faultfinders, Irritants are essential to the perfection of others, for in their company we're forced to learn patience and tolerance. Although it's important not to buy into the Irritant's innate pessimism, we must also be nonjudgmental. We must remember that Irritants are perfecting their themes so that we can perfect ours through them.

20. Justice. Many of America's Founding Fathers, concerned as they were with fairness and equality, are examples of the Justice theme in operation, as are those who eagerly give their names when they've witnessed an accident or crime. As admirable as all this sounds, it's imperative that these souls use discretion in their choices and remain God-centered.

21. Lawfulness. Practicing or teaching law are obvious choices for those in this category, who are almost obsessed with issues of legality, while others may be found serving on governing boards. When elevated, people with this theme keep the world safe and balanced, but they must always be on guard against the possibility of using their power in a self-serving manner.

22. Leader. Those with this theme are self-controlled, premeditated, and rarely innovative, choosing to take charge in areas that are already established. Their drive is toward success rather than creation, and their challenge is to avoid "power trips."

23. Loner. Although often in the vanguard of society, those with the theme of Loner invariably pick occupations or situations in which they're isolated in some way. (This is a secondary theme of mine, for being a psychic has set me apart from others.) Loners are generally happy with themselves but should watch their irritation levels when people come into their space. If each theme recognizes the presence and significance of others, the result will be far greater tolerance and understanding in the world, and—eventually—peace.

24. Loser. Losers are extremely negative, although unlike those with the Fallibility theme, they're born without handicaps. Often Losers have many good points, but they choose to ignore them. Although their theme may resemble that of the Irritant in their proclivity for constant criticism, they're different in that they invariably place the blame back on "poor me." Losers are prime martyrs, moving from one elaborate soap opera to another.

It's important that we not judge the people who have this theme, remembering that their patterns were chosen to enable us to perfect ourselves—and by observing them in action, we'll endeavor to be more positive.

25. Manipulator. This is one of the most powerful themes, for Manipulators are easily able to control situations as well as people. By viewing life as a chessboard, those with this theme can move individuals and circumstances to their advantage, as though they're pawns. (President Franklin Roosevelt was a prime example of a Manipulator in action.) When such a person works for the good of others, this theme is elevated to its highest purpose. However, when the theme is misused, the ultimate goal of perfection takes a long time to achieve.

26. Passivity. Surprisingly, those with a Passivity theme are actually active—but about nothing. Although they'll take stands on issues at times, it's always in a non-violent manner. Of course any extreme is hurtful to the individual, but *some* tension may be needed in order to bring about the perfection of the soul.

27. Patience. The Patience theme is clearly one of the most difficult paths to perfection, as those in this category seem to desire a more rapid attainment than those with less challenging themes. Often, they carry great amounts of guilt when they feel that they've strayed from their goal, resulting in their impatience. This attitude can lead to self-abasement and suppressed anger. These souls must be lenient with themselves, for it's difficult enough living through the circumstances that they've chosen in order to express this theme.

28. Pawn. Whether the means are negative or positive, Pawns trigger something of great magnitude into being (the biblical Judas is a classic example of this theme). We can't evolve toward universal perfection without the Pawn, but those who select this theme should preserve their dignity by only picking worthy causes.

29. Peacemaker. Those who select the theme of Peacemaker aren't as tranquil as the name implies. Peacemakers are actually pushy in their desire for, and pursuit of, peace—they work endlessly to stop violence and war, addressing a larger audience than those who've opted for Harmony as a theme. And their goal of peace far exceeds an allegiance to one particular group or country.

30. Perfectionist. We should all want things clean and orderly in our lives, yet those with this theme can go that extra step and be very innovative at work, thus saving time and money. Perfectionists also tend to be harder on themselves than anyone else. They demand that they do everything just right, with no opening for sloppiness. If it gets to the point that this becomes an obsessive or compulsive problem, then this theme has to be tempered. Perfectionists may have to force themselves to leave their work or responsibilities and kick back for a time to rejuvenate themselves.

31. Performance. Those with a Performance theme find it highly rewarding but frequently exhausting. These souls are the true "party animals"—some will go into actual entertainment careers, but others will simply be content to entertain in their homes or offices. The challenge here is for those with Performance as a theme to

combat burnout by looking within, thus acquiring the ability to nourish and entertain *themselves.*

32. Persecution. People with this theme live their lives in anticipation of the worst, certain that they're being singled out for persecution. Experiencing pleasure can throw them into a panic because they're convinced that somehow they must pay for it. This arduous theme is chosen to allow others to grow spiritually.

33. Persecutor. Those with a Persecutor theme may range from wife beaters and child abusers to mass murderers. It's difficult to see the purpose of this theme within a single life span, but these seemingly "bad seeds" have a self-chosen role to play that enables humankind to evolve toward perfection. Once again, it's imperative that we don't judge individuals with this theme.

34. Poverty. The theme of Poverty appears most frequently in developing nations, yet it can be even more of a challenge in affluent societies. Some of those with Poverty as a theme may even have all they need to be comfortable and yet *feel* poor. With progress, the frenzy fades and is slowly replaced by a sense of bliss as the realization comes that the trappings of this world are transitory things whose importance will quickly pass.

35. Psychic. The theme of the Psychic is more a challenge than a gift, at least in the early stages. Those with this theme often come from strict backgrounds where authority figures strive to deny or suppress their gifts of being able to hear, see, or sense things in a manner beyond that of "normal" perception. Eventually, these souls will learn to accept and live with their abilities, using them for good in a spiritual, if not professional, manner. (Incidentally, I don't carry this theme; psychic ability has never been a challenge point in my life.)

36. Rejection. This challenging theme manifests itself early, accelerating with the entry into school and subsequent involvement in relationships. Often these individuals are deserted by those they love—even their own children will adopt surrogate mother or father figures. The pattern can be broken once the person recognizes what's happening and surrenders the action and ego involvement to God.

37. Rescuer. One often finds the Rescuer working alongside the Cause Fighter, but when the Cause Fighter moves on to another crusade, the Rescuer remains to care for the injured party. Someone with a Rescuer theme has a high degree of empathy and can manifest strength for those in need. Even when others have obviously created their own problems, the Rescuer is determined to "save" them. By doing so, the Rescuer is often the one who gets hurt. This theme presents a tough road to travel, but the spiritual rewards are great indeed.

38. Responsibility. Individuals who have chosen the Responsibility theme embrace it with fervor rather than obligation, and they feel guilty if they don't take care of everyone who comes into their orbit. The challenge is to decide what is immediate and necessary and then to stand back and allow others to share in the assumption of responsibilities.

39. Spirituality. The quest to find a spiritual center is an all-encompassing one for those pursuing the Spirituality theme. (We find it in people such as Billy Graham and Mother Teresa, along with laypeople who give their lives, money, or time to contribute to humankind.) When the full potential of this theme has been reached, these souls become farsighted, compassionate, and magnanimous; but while still involved in the search, they must guard against being narrow and judgmental in their views.

40. Survival. For any number of reasons, real or imagined, life is a constant struggle for those who've selected a Survival theme. At their best in a crisis situation, these souls take a grim view of day-to-day existence. The obvious challenge here is to lighten up.

41. Temperance. The challenge here is to avoid extremes; those with a Temperance theme are more than likely dealing with an addiction of one kind or another. Or they may have conquered the actual addiction but are still dealing with residual feelings about it. The key to combating the fanaticism that often characterizes this theme is moderation . . . the true meaning of temperance.

42. Tolerance. Those choosing this theme must be tolerant about everything—world affairs, relatives, children, politics, and so forth. Their burden is so great that they'll often only select one area to tolerate, remaining very narrow-minded about all the rest. But by recognizing their theme, these souls can meet the challenge and grow more magnanimous in the process.

43. Victim. These souls have chosen to be martyrs and sacrificial lambs. By their example—dramatically displayed by the media—we're made aware of injustice. (John F. Kennedy is one who pursued a Victim theme through his means of exit, his back pain, his family name, and the pressures placed upon him by his parents.) After having played their parts, many Victims may choose to rewrite future scripts by altering their masochistic tendencies.

44. Victimizer. People's Temple leader Jim Jones was a prime example of this theme in action—it's obvious that many lives, as well as many life themes, interacted with his. In the tapestry of life, Jones's unique role may have been to focus public attention on cult abuses.

45. Warrior. Those with this theme are fearless risk takers who assume a variety of physical challenges. Many go into some form of military service or law enforcement, and if they have Humanitarian as a secondary theme, they may be particularly effective. Although it's important to temper aggression, it still remains that without Warriors, we would be prey to tyrants.

46. Wealth. This theme sounds like a great choice, but it's invariably more like a burden that leads to destructive behavior if left unchecked. As with any theme, its goal is to overcome its negative aspects. Wealth is a seductive temptress that acts like an addiction—it's very difficult to gain control of this theme, so it tends to become one's master. People with this theme may be obsessed with acquiring, growing, and hoarding money, unconcerned with the methods of acquisition or the consequences of

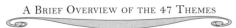

their actions in their quest for more. Moral values are of no importance to this theme, so it can take many lives to overcome due to its powerful effect on a person. When people do finally master Wealth, then you find them freely giving away their belongings, with no desire for anything in return.

47. Winner. Unlike those with the theme of Infallibility, to whom everything comes easily, Winners strive to win with great tenacity, often gambling or entering contests. Perennial optimists, they're always certain that the next deal, job, or marriage will be the best. No sooner has one deal fallen through than they pick themselves up and go on to what they know will be a winning situation. Dwight Eisenhower was a positive example of this theme. As a general, his unfailing optimism was inspiring; as a President, his confidence had a calming effect. The challenge for these souls, which Eisenhower appears to have met, is to take a realistic approach to winning.

In all the years I've talked to people and told them their themes, they invariably say, "That's me . . . that's exactly who I am!" Yet each of us actually has bits and pieces of all the themes because we've lived multiple lives.

Please don't act as if themes are astrological signs by trying to find out the themes of everyone around you to see if you get along. Different categories can get along with almost any other, because we'll always learn something to help our souls perfect.

Now some people become confused when they feel that they're victims of their charts. No, we're always

acquiring spiritual knowledge, especially from other people. For example, my abusive first husband helped awaken my soul's strength, and I learned that no one had the right to defame or hurt me.

While there are places for battered women to go these days, back then they didn't, so I took my kids and lived in a tenement. We ate a lot of pork and beans, and I kept teaching. I only made $455 a month—and after rent, utilities, and food and clothing for three kids, I almost didn't make it. But with faith and prayer, something would always come up to help. I did readings and crafts . . . anything to make my way. My friends and family stuck close together, and strange as it may seem, we all look back on those times as some of our happiest. The main thing was that my kids and I were free of the screaming and abuse.

I'd like to end this chapter by emphasizing that you don't have to know your themes to make your relationships work—it's just a way of understanding or explaining why they sometimes do or don't. Sure, the more you explore these themes, the more you can pick out your own and that of others, but as I've said so many times, the bottom line is this: If you don't have spirituality *and* the love of God and humankind, no relationship will ever work, no matter whom you're with or what their themes are.

♔ ♔ ♔

Chapter Nine

RELATIONSHIP CHALLENGES

*A*s all 47 of the life themes overlap, I'm not going to discuss every single one in detail. Instead, I'd rather focus on how they interact, especially since this is a relationship book. In this chapter, I'm going to look at how some themes may find each other challenging.

I'd like to stress that by writing about the importance of themes in relationships, I'm just trying to show why some individuals might not make it together. If they know how, people can elevate their themes so that they not only get along better, but perfect their themes *with* their partners. Even those of us with the same themes can get along together if we modify our behavior. As corny as it seems, it's almost like the premise of "We both go hand in hand to spiritually obtain our perfection." It's a combination of sharing and sacrifice—to share together whenever possible, and to sacrifice our needs for our partners' when necessary.

The themes guide our purposes *and* the facets of our personality that we add onto from life after life of incarnations. By looking closely at the themes, we can also lock them into our personality traits, such as cranky, jealous, angry, disturbed, depressed, psychotic, eccentric, jovial, lazy, moody, optimistic, pessimistic, and so forth. These fit into all themes, whether Harmony, Irritant, Manipulator, Builder, or what have you.

Personality vs. Themes

What are our personalities anyway? Well, along with our outward personas, they're also the sum total of who we are, what we've acquired through our original essence that came from God, and the marvelous add-ons that we've picked up from past lives. We basically remain the same core essence, but living multiple existences helps us make our essence better. When we go back to the Other Side after a particular life, we have the ability to correct some of the flaws from that existence and try coming to Earth again in order to ascend to being a better soul.

There are many personality traits that are wonderful and others that are unbelievable, such as the angry or always jealous person, or even the constant talkers who bore you silly. There's someone in my life who loves to ramble on about herself—long, boring, drawn-out stories that have no bearing on anything. But since my theme is Humanitarian (which we'll get into later), I feel sorry for her and realize that no one else wants to listen to her at all.

Similarly, I knew this guy who was just like her, and his conversations always went something like this: "I went to buy a pair of shoes on Sunday . . . no, wait, it was Monday. No . . . it *was* Sunday because it was raining. I went to Nordstrom first . . . no, that's not right—it was Macy's . . . I'd parked closer to Macy's and said to myself, *Well, since I'm closer I might as well go in Macy's first.*"

I won't torture you anymore, but he would go on and on until I found myself trying not to scream out what was going through my head: *For God's sake, get to the point! Did you get the shoes or not? And who the hell cares?*

Again, anything taken to the extreme becomes impossible to deal with. Years ago I'd been dating one of those talkers when I then met a very quiet man. At first I was elated to just have the silence, but then I realized that this wasn't any good either. When I asked the quiet one about it, his reply was, "I only talk when I have something important to say." Well, apparently he *never* had anything important to say.

What happened to the art of conversation? Like many of you, I remember that after church on Sunday my family and I would have dinner; and our friends and relatives would spend hours at the table talking about the news, politics, what we did during the week . . . it was a feast of listening, chatting, and learning. That's why my favorite thing to do in the whole world is to have a meal with people who are alive with fun, jokes, and interesting conversation.

My grandmother was the best storyteller ever. Every yarn she spun was interesting, suspenseful, and delivered a moral, and then she and I would discuss it. This society doesn't do that anymore—we've become so isolated in our homes and jobs that hardly any new information can come in. It's like listening to the same newscast over and over again.

I'm reminded of this couple who came to see me for a reading. They'd been married for 55 years, and when she'd ask a question, he'd smile and nod; then it was his turn, and she'd smile and nod. Not once did they contradict each other or put each other down. As they were leaving, they both said that they never got tired of talking to each other and exploring new books and ideas together. Almost in unison, they both said, "He/she is my best friend." What a God-given blessing that is—and it can be that way for us if we're simply cognizant of the person we're involved with.

Now my all-time least favorite personality is the lazy one. These people can't act, and what's even more exhausting, they simply won't. Oh, they might give it a try if they're screamed at enough, but who has the energy and will to constantly do this? For example, I find it unacceptable for a husband to sit around and watch TV all day while his wife works. Nevertheless, I often see women putting up with such "deadbeats" just to say they're married. I say get a dog or cat—at least pets give you something back! By the same token, the husband who works hard for his family has a right to expect a clean home and dinner on the table. I raised many children, yet I always kept my house neat and prepared the meals. If everyone pitches in, things stay in a semblance of order.

I'm convinced that laziness is a real character defect. Life is meant to be experienced, not observed. If that's what you wanted, you would have been better off just staying on the Other Side.

Learning from the Themes

The primary theme is what we are; that is, the basis of our souls and the driving force of our lives. The secondary theme is what we're here to perfect, entering into our lives constantly so that we may learn from it. In most instances, souls learn from both themes—especially now—because the reincarnation schematic is coming to a close. Even though we change themes and relationships in each life, we still keep our original essence and basic personality intact throughout all of our lives.

No matter what themes we have, it can be hard. Then when you add in other relationships with their themes and past-life influences (let alone influences from *this* life), it's a wonder that we ever relate to anyone else. That's why I keep repeating that the more spiritual we are, the more we understand and love each other, resulting in wonderful connections with our fellow humans.

Of course, any theme or purpose that you come in with should never be taken to the extreme because then it defeats the purpose of your learning. As Jesus wondered, "What does it profit a man to gain the whole world and lose his soul?" Ask yourself just how far you're willing to go to sacrifice yourself or your learning ability for the sake of just saying that you have someone in your life. You have to strike an acceptable balance, and sometimes that can take years to achieve.

In addition, if you let the problems of this (or any) life take precedence, you can sabotage any relationship. You don't have to bring your past experiences into your current relationships—you can cut through the negativity in yourself and others.

Naturally, nothing is perfect. Being human, often we feel that we'd like to strangle our partners, but that's just stress and frustration talking. It takes two to fight, so sometimes it's better to just walk away when having an argument. This isn't ignoring the problem; you're simply waiting for your partner to calm down. But don't carry this too far by walking away from *every* issue. As my grandmother used to say, "Never go to bed mad, because

the problem won't magically evaporate with the morning light." Instead, you'll wake up in a bad mood and walk around all day in a funk.

So, getting back to our themes, I'd like to take a look at a few of them and their individual challenges. Here they are, in no particular order:

— The **Analyzer** theme, which you can see in scientists and others in high-tech fields, is great unless it's carried to its opposite polarity (like any other theme). Trying to understand the "why" of everything is fine, because Analyzers learn wonderful things; but picking apart each word, gesture, or circumstance in life as if it's under a high-powered microscope becomes exhausting for those around these souls.

If you're perfecting patience, maybe you can put up with the Analyzer, but the continual questioning, such as, "What do you mean when you do such-and-such or say this or that?" can drive you away. If you're an Analyzer, try to accept life as it is. Sure, people want to learn, but if you tear all the petals off the flower, you just have a naked stem and miss the beauty of how things exist as they are.

— The **Aesthetic Pursuits** theme encompasses those who have an affinity for literature and the arts, such as music, acting, dance, painting, writing, and singing. This theme reveals itself very early. My granddaughter, for instance, demonstrated signs that she loved to write even before she could form spoken words. These people are driven by their innate talents, and they won't settle for anything less than to be on Broadway; or become a recording artist, painter, actor, dancer, or writer.

Sadly, this hunger for the limelight tends to lead to the neglect of relationships. In its lower state, this theme can cause a type of false ego-love of self. Aesthetics feel that no one person can fill their hearts like the adoration of the crowd can. Their partners then feel left out because their loved ones are getting all the adoration, causing them to take a backseat. The themes of Tolerance and Patience go well with Aesthetic Pursuits, but someone who's with a star has to be fully ensconced in their own God-center and know who they are. The celebrities I read for (of course I won't name them) are often the most insecure people—their love affair is truly with the public.

— The **Emotionality** theme can be a challenge if (like any theme) you *become* it rather than learn from it. In other words, if everything upsets you, then no one will be able to take your constant drama. Since Builders are practical and stable, they can help because they bring balance and help others construct their lives, one block at a time.

However, if those with the Emotionality theme are too far into their feelings, they may need some medical help to stabilize them. As I've often said, while emotion is the activator, it shouldn't be used as an excuse to be a diva.

— Those with the **Performance** theme don't necessarily *need* to go into show business, like those with that of Aesthetic Pursuits do (but they certainly can). Instead, they tend to be the "life of the party." They always have jokes, stories, or songs to share . . . anything to entertain a crowd. In its elevated state, people with this theme are delightful and fun and will be invited everywhere because

of their sparkling personalities. And many of these individuals are content to simply be upbeat and entertain at their homes or offices. Who wouldn't want to be around such happy, positive people?

This theme may find it difficult to fight burnout—even though all they need do is look within, thus acquiring the ability to nourish and be happy within themselves. And since our lives move so fast now, we sadly don't have the "old cracker-barrel days" anymore. Those were when men in the old mercantile stores would gather around the stove or cracker barrel and recycle stories to perform and entertain.

People with the Performance theme can be great friends, especially if they take more of a low-key approach and are pleasant and amiable rather than rambunctious bores. Analyzers or Controllers work well with them because they offer balance and some kind of ability to stabilize the overworked need to entertain.

— Individuals with the **Harmony** theme want everyone to be happy, and it defies their very essence to be with anyone who's miserable. Consequently, they won't make it with Irritants. They also don't get along well with Manipulators, who want to control every situation around them—people included. And since those with the Harmony theme want to make things right, they'll try to give estimation to someone with the Infallibility or Controller themes. I don't want to say that it's useless, but these relationships can be incredibly difficult.

— The **Manipulator** can't even get along with the **Controller** because it would always be a contest to see who wins! Both of these themes have to be in charge all

the time, which seems exhausting to me, yet they appear to thrive on taking over other people's lives and getting them to bow to their will. Usually the Manipulator theme can be found in a blackmail-type situation, such as, "If you don't do what I say, you won't get my love or money, and I may even kick you out of the family." It's also seen in work situations in which employees are threatened with losing their jobs if they don't do as their co-workers say. And some women are trapped in bad marriages because they have no other means of financial support unless they abide by their manipulating or controlling husbands.

⋯⋅◈⋅⋯

Now while it seems as if this is a negative theme, we can't judge these individuals. Themes can always be modified, just as we use anger-management classes to turn a negative into a positive. We must also remember that all of us have tiny bits of every theme inside of us, thanks to our past lives. In addition, many themes that seem to be negative, such as the Controller or Manipulator, can be used for a higher purpose . . . which actually makes them quite positive.

Many of the "kinder and gentler" themes have their own thorns, too. For example, even the Caretaker theme can be taken too far, to the point that these individuals take care of others to the exclusion of themselves or their own families.

— The **Caretaker, Humanitarian,** and **Rescuer** are all sisters, and their challenges can be more internal than external. These three seemingly unselfish themes can be very hard on the people associated with them, and these givers can become immobilized—they're so drained and spread thin that there isn't anything left for themselves or their loved ones. I have the Humanitarian theme, for instance, and it took me some years before I realized that I couldn't always be all things to all people, no matter how much I wanted to be.

I love my fellow human beings; and through my teaching, writing, lectures, and media appearances, I've always tried to honestly help others with their problems. I've made mistakes and encountered pitfalls along the way, but what I really had to learn is that if I never stop myself, I'll burn out and become so used up that I can't do anything for anyone. It never came to me so pointedly until I was walking through my office one day and heard one of my dear associates on the phone, saying something to the effect of, "Yes, I know you have a problem and I'll get you in as soon as I can, but if we gave Sylvia everyone who needed her right when they needed her, there wouldn't be any more Sylvia. After all, there's only one of her here."

I thought about that and began to review the last several years—they had been a barrage of criminal cases, readings, media appearances, lectures, and even late-night calls from police departments. That's when I began to prioritize for my sanity and health's sake. I still get to thousands of people because I love what I do so much, but now I give myself some time off just to write (which relaxes me), do needlepoint, and spend the day with my family.

If you relate to the theme of Caretaker, Humanitarian, or Rescuer, relationships can be hard because of the time you devote to helping others. Your spouse or kids

will often wonder, "What about us?" And many times, no matter what you do, it's not enough, for they want your undivided attention.

These categories don't necessarily have to stick together, for they also do well with those with the Builder, Harmony, or Justice themes. If you choose to be in a relationship with someone with any of these themes, you can get along quite well if you both have the same focus to help people, but you must ensure that he or she slows down enough to take time for you *and* him- or herself.

— **Rescuers** are probably the most stubbornly purposeful of all of the themes. If they don't take care, they'll save you—whether you want or need to be saved—and then direct you toward their idea of what will make you happy. In its moderate stage, individuals with this theme want to reinvent you or are great at interventions, but they don't seem to be able to rescue *themselves*. However, in its elevated form, this theme manifests itself as the successful city doctor who goes to a small town, or a person who starts a school in the ghetto. Father Flanagan (the founder of Girls and Boys Town) was a wonderful example of the elevated Rescuer.

— The theme of **Follower** isn't bad unto itself, but it's one that you have to be very watchful of, for it can lead you into being controlled and manipulated by a person who professes to be perfect. Then there's the **Fallibility** theme, which is often so full of humility and scrupulousness that those with it can be very aggravating. Their way of always humbly being wrong can make you crazy . . . to the point that you want to say, "Quit wallowing in your own pain and sense of guilt!" This person is always

obsessing about how unworthy he or she is. Oftentimes individuals with these two themes are sitting ducks, as we used to say, or prey for those with the Infallibility, Controller, or Manipulator themes, who are only out for themselves.

It's important that if you have a Follower or Fallibility theme, you understand that you can't use being with these people to improve your karma—as soon as you realize what you've gotten yourself into, get what you need from the situation and then get out. You learn nothing from going down the tubes with individuals who control and drain you.

— Within their theme, **Persecutors** often tend to oppress others' causes. Since these are the abusers, mass killers, or torturers, it can be difficult to understand them, but they're here to help us learn. After all, if we don't have the dark side, we can't perfect our lives and our spirituality. Those with this theme don't tend to have any lasting relationships; the ones they do have are usually transient and violent, either physically or verbally. If they could just lead Christlike lives, they'd never think of condemning other people. The only individuals Jesus ever spoke out against were the Pharisees (hypocrites who preached one way and acted another).

— On the other side of the coin, those with the **Persecution** theme spend their lives anticipating the worst. They're sure that whatever happens is directed at them, and they also believe that they're cursed, which of course isn't true.

If you have this theme, it can be very hard for you to have a relationship with anyone, unless it's someone

with a strong spiritual theme of Tolerance and Rescuer, but even then it can wear very thin. Just remember that all themes are designed to allow us to grow spiritually—so taking a harsh one means that you chose to perfect over it, not sink into it.

— Those with the **Loser** theme can have good points, but they often choose to ignore them. Unlike the Persecution theme, you'll find them going out of their way to create drama, and they also seem to put themselves in harm's way. When we buy a lottery ticket, most of us usually don't give it much thought when we don't win. But the Loser will say, "I don't know why I bought that ticket in the first place—nothing good ever happens to me." What's more amazing is that if something good ever does happen to them, they'll sabotage it.

Unfortunately, women are pulled in by Losers more than men are. Look at the gals who want to marry prisoners. There's something in the female makeup (besides their individual themes) that wants to mother or make better. Yet you can't form a viable relationship with a Loser. I don't think that even those with the Persecution theme could stand them, for they'd be vying for the title of "who has it worse." We all know these people, and as emotionally trying as they can be, we should endeavor to be as kind to them as possible. But we shouldn't hang around them too much, since negativity begets negativity.

Again, try not to judge, for you must look at these people as those to learn from. However, perfecting doesn't mean that you have to rescue them (they wouldn't let you anyway). And remember, if you feel that you have this theme, you can work to overcome it. Enhancing your relationship with God will keep it in check.

— Unlike Losers, those with the theme of **Rejection** really do seem to be spurned, no matter what. Now it's true that all themes work from our internal feelings, which then manifest in our outward reality, but these souls seemingly can't do anything right. Whether it's the way they look or act, they feel rejected, and this inclination tends to start in childhood. Again, like so many themes, once the pattern or lesson has been learned, it can be broken, and then the false ego can be surrendered. But this will only happen if the person gets tired of being scorned and genuinely wants the pattern to end.

People with this theme are good with Activators, who can have so much going for them that they take the individuals who feel rejection right out of themselves.

— The **Loner** is also a difficult theme if (like all of them) you don't work with it. Now, while my primary theme is Humanitarian, Loner is my secondary theme. Many times themes are opposite of each other. That's obviously the case with me, for how could you be in the public eye and still be a loner?

After much soul searching, it dawned on me that my psychic abilities sometimes isolate me. The fact that I have this gift that is frequently misunderstood often puts me in a lonely place. I've never felt alone—but again, it's one's frame of mind or essence that emanates from the theme. I also believe that people who are private have the Loner theme. Yes, my *life* is an open book, but my *mind* isn't, and perhaps I'm more aware of that than others who don't have this theme are.

I've learned to deal with this theme and reconcile it with my Humanitarian one—my writing, reading, and researching give me my alone time, and then I go out and enjoy being in public.

— Those with the **Passivity** theme may be so non-committal that they seem lazy. Actually, they just don't have that much passion for life. They'd make good monks if they could get it together to enter the monastery, since if they do take a stand on any issue, it's always in a non-violent way.

I remember when my friend Bob Williams and I encountered some of these people in groups in the '60s at various gatherings. They weren't the Cause Fighters, Banner Carriers, or Warriors—they seemed to simply want life to pass, thus allowing them to live removed from everyday worries. They wanted to be different; but what amazed me was that they all dressed, talked, and looked alike.

There are some themes I don't understand, and Passivity really baffles me. The vision of a holy man meditating on a rock comes to mind here. I always want to say, "Come down and get busy helping others, as Jesus did," but we have to be tolerant of everyone's path. Just because we personally don't agree with something doesn't make it wrong. As long as difficult-to-understand individuals don't harm anybody else, I feel that they should be allowed to live and perfect in the way they feel is right.

An Activator or Catalyst could help someone with the Passive theme by giving him or her a cause to get excited about.

— The theme of **Patience** is one that many relate to, yet it's one of the more difficult paths to perfection. Individuals with this theme can become very scrupulous, even about themselves, because they often feel guilt when they're impatient with their children, family, co-workers, and so forth. Yet they can become easily annoyed over every little thing—their partners always need to be on time, the trash must be taken out immediately, or the grass has to be cut now. Everything is in the *now*. The person with this theme should meditate, take deep breaths, and realize that all things take time. (I'm reminded of the car that speeds past you, only to meet up with you at the next stoplight.) Try being lenient with yourself and others, and keep repeating: *It will all get done in its own time*—obsessing about things only causes stress, and stress causes illness. And while there are many "nows" in life, they don't always have to be *your* now.

People with the theme of Patience will constantly have it tested, which of course is the reason it's so hard. If they can overcome their themes, such individuals can be some of the kindest and gentlest in the world, making great friends and spouses for those of us who tend to not be so patient. They also seem to be wonderful listeners and can settle down those of us who are more emotional. Patience goes well with the Activator, Catalyst, and Experiencer because those with these themes are more immediate and usually do things rapidly and on time.

— The theme of **Tolerance**, although similar in some respects to that of Patience, is more accentuated, for it goes deeper and wider in scope. In its lowest aspect, this form can almost be opposed to itself and turn *in*tolerant, causing those who have it to become bigoted or prejudiced. It may seem rather obvious, but having this theme means that the individuals must learn to tolerate life's obstacles, the defects in themselves and others, and people with different points of view. This doesn't mean that they ever have to stand back and sanction cruelty, injustices, or inequities, but this theme truly typifies the phrase "Live and let live."

Notice that it isn't just those of us with the Patience or Tolerance themes who can be put off by individual habits or idiosyncrasies. My all-time favorite is someone snapping and chewing gum, but another winner is someone who smacks their lips or sucks their teeth while eating. I also have a friend who makes this horrible snuffing sound with her nose—I can put up with it if I'm in a patient mood, but after an hour or so, I've had enough. I guess I've learned to tolerate human beings themselves more than their habits.

Keep in mind that people's idiosyncrasies have nothing to do with their colors, creeds, or politics. Who are we to judge someone else's way of life or belief system? We must always remember that Jesus said, "Judge not, lest ye be judged."

— The theme of **Poverty** can really drive everyone around you crazy. While this can occur in developing nations, I've found that poor people in Turkey, Africa, Greece, Mexico, and other countries are often not even aware that they're poverty stricken. It seems that Americans are more aware and judgmental of the poor, turning a deaf ear or an unseeing eye to their plight.

All themes are internal and can become a mind-set those with the Poverty theme many times have the fear of not having enough or ending up on the street homeless. It can even be that they're financially comfortable yet feel poor, or they have an abundance of money and fear poverty to the point that they become miserly. And my grandmother used to say, "Often when poverty comes through the window, love flies out the door." This is tragic but true.

The Poverty theme goes well with Survivors or Winners because they assail fears by overcoming obstacles and bringing in money.

— The **Responsibility** theme sounds wonderful, but it's actually very difficult. It's also the counterpart to the Humanitarian and Rescuer. The person with this theme feels responsible for everything and everyone, oftentimes to the point of neglecting those around them. They feel like they have to "chicken soup" everyone who comes into their space, and they're the ones who raise their hands immediately when someone asks for a volunteer.

This theme can be great in moderation, but it may also lead to the neglect of family and friends. For example, I had a reading with a man who said that his wife's volunteer work and obligations to the community were praiseworthy, but they were causing her to sacrifice her family's relationships. Yes, it's laudable to help others, but we have to choose our priorities. If we let our family or loved ones go begging, praise from the outside will seem pretty hollow.

If you have the Responsibility theme, then your challenge is to decide what's really important to you and yours, and then be able to stand back and clap when someone else can step in. You'll do well in a relationship with someone with the Justice theme, for he or she can bring balance to your life. The Peacemaker is also a good choice, for he or she will provide a balance of humanity as well as humility.

— **Justice** also sounds like a great theme, but these people can be hard to live with if you don't have the same interests. The reason is that they see so much injustice in this world that it almost makes them rattled. They have to realize that they can't fix the whole world, but they *can* do it inside for God and for the circle of people around them.

— The theme of **Peacemaker** isn't as specific as it seems. Unlike Cause Fighters, souls with this theme usually use a larger canvas of opportunity to display what they feel is right, and they generally need a wide audience to get their views across.

Most of us can't bear the ugliness in the world, but Peacemakers feel that it's their duty to make peace *everywhere*. They'll get into politics and become members of organizations such as Greenpeace, and they'll be driven to rally people to follow their lead. They can also be great orators.

It's very important that Peacemakers remain in touch with their families and loved ones, much like those with the Responsibility theme. They get along with the gentler Harmony theme, or with the Lawfulness theme that fits well but has more intellectual control.

— Those in the **Lawfulness** category can be just as active as those with the Justice, Cause Fighter, and Banner Carrier themes, except that the former is almost obsessed by issues of legality. People with this theme are in service to others and are concerned with keeping the world safe, such as law-enforcement officers, lawyers, firefighters, or those on governing boards. This is just fine unless they get too power hungry and become self-serving . . . but I've very rarely seen this happen, since people with this theme tend to be so busy serving the public good and working to make society safe that they don't have time to be self-aggrandizing.

— Those with the **Spirituality** theme can be very driven—but also quite farsighted, compassionate, and magnanimous. While the rewards of their search can sometimes be marvelous, such individuals may also be myopic in the pursuit of spiritual fulfillment. If they're not careful, they can even be pulled into the occult.

— The **Pawn** can be one of the most confusing of the themes, especially in relationships. Individuals with this theme can create a situation or jump into one that's already in place and trigger reactions. They're convinced that they must be "the fuse," and in most cases, they are. These individuals have a difficult time finding and keeping relationships because most people don't understand their obsessions. Gandhi, for instance, was a Pawn, and his obsession was so great that he was ready to starve for it. Even his wife and children were relegated to the background as he pursued his all-consuming need to trigger economic freedom and independence for India.

Pawns can get along with those with the Aesthetic Pursuits theme because they have their own agendas to advance and will leave the Pawns to do their own thing.

— At first glance, the theme of **Survival** seems to be more understandable in the sense that we're *all* survivors in this learning place of a planet, but this theme is far more specific than that. Yes, we all survive, but those with this theme make it a focal point to do so *at all costs*. In its elevated form, these souls make it through every hardship and help others do the same—they can be heroes in war and head up peace groups. Unlike the Cause Fighter or Banner Carrier, they don't feel that they're fighting for a cause, but are simply overcoming adversities. They can

also be very positive and purposeful, believing that they can surmount any odds (and they usually do). Even if they're thwarted, they'll still make it over, through, or around that obstacle.

Individuals with this theme can also become good businesspeople and strive to become successful in many fields. It's not unusual, like the Catalyst, to have many occupations successfully going at the same time. However, in its lower form, the Survival theme can cause people to be miserly and determined to make it regardless of how they have to do it. They can even fall into criminal actions or use any means necessary to ensure that they'll be all right.

If you're involved with a person who has the Survival theme, it works well if you let him or her take the reins, but if your partner feels as if you're holding him or her back, you'll be history. I was married to someone with this theme . . . enough said. The Humanitarian doesn't do well with surviving at all costs. This isn't a criticism—it's just a bad mix. The Passive theme works well here because the person with the Survival theme will take care of them both. The theme of Caretaker also goes well because this person gives the survivor some TLC. And Builders are a good match because they get behind the survivors and help them fulfill their goals.

— The theme of **Temperance** can be particularly difficult because it demands so much of the individual. People with this theme tend to take or do everything to the extreme. This can relate to drugs, alcohol, gambling, or sex; it can be in the ultimate obsession to succeed, to be a workaholic to the extreme; or their ferocious need to produce art, music, or work of any kind. Whatever they can't seem to do in moderation can take over their entire lives and become a love affair in its own right.

Those with this theme can have a hard time finding others to share their lives with because they tend to take pleasure in creating chaos. Yet some people can be addicted to drama, negativity, or even being martyrs. If the Temperance theme is elevated, those in this category will do well with the Harmony or Perfection themes, as all desire the semblance of sanity in life.

— The theme of **Victim** is also a difficult one to come in with, and it's sometimes even harder to be around. It's true that some highly elevated souls come in to be sacrificed for a greater good—for example, the women who were burned as witches took this theme to eventually show the world what happens when religion and mass hysteria get out of hand. Joan of Arc was a victim of the highest order—she led France to one victory after another, but because she heard voices, she was also burned at the stake. Another tragic example was that of the millions of Jews (and some of my distant relatives) who were slaughtered at the hands of the Adolf Hitler–led Nazis. These are the saints who made the world realize what an evil dictator can do to innocent people.

Unfortunately, the lesser part of this theme relates to the martyrs, who feel that the world is against them and who wallow in self-pity. No matter what happens, Victims are certain that they've been targeted. They feel guilty for everything, even going so far as to look for people or situations to take them down and feed into their poor estimation of themselves.

It's hard for most of us to understand that there are some with this theme who just sink right into it, rather than overcoming it. Of course, as I've said, this can happen with all themes, for they're to be learned from and overcome or elevated—and, unfortunately, some aren't up to the task. So if you have this theme, try to look at life with joy rather than the supposition that everyone is out to get you.

Finding a relationship for those with the Victim theme can be very difficult, since every action that anyone performs can be mistaken as a direct assault on them. However, they *can* go well with Analyzers because they can help Victims sort out why they feel this way. Experiencers can also show them different vistas in life that take their minds off themselves.

— The **Victimizer** theme is a very dark one, and if it isn't overcome, can lead to the person becoming a killer or stalker. And if they don't do their victimizing in a physical way, they can do it mentally, which can be just as hard and scar just as deeply.

I've actually only encountered one person with this theme; I met him in passing at a police station in Seattle. He asked me to tell him what was going to happen to him. (He was going to get life in prison.) He had no remorse of any kind; he was just concerned about himself and what was going to happen to him. So, unlike other themes—which are interested in love, finances, and whether or not they're doing the right thing or are on track—Victimizers only care if they'll be hurt.

The theme of Victimizer might seemingly go well with Victims, but it seems that this is too easy for them—probably sensing that they're already too victimized by themselves so there wouldn't be much challenge in going after those who are already unworthy and having a pity party. Unfortunately, Rescuers can get caught in the feeling that they can save this type of person. Followers also have to be careful of becoming enamored with these often charismatic and convincing individuals.

Again, I realize that these themes can be difficult to understand, but from them we learn what *not* to be and hopefully become kinder in the process. Sometimes it's a good thing to have a negative example to help us turn the other way to a better and healthier relationship.

Also, my grandmother used to say, "Fortunately—or sometimes unfortunately—there can be someone for everyone." That's not necessarily a good thing, but if you look around, the strangest combinations can occur, but they're always for our souls' perfection. Every connection we make goes toward understanding something that we don't always discern in this life—maybe it won't be until we get back to the Other Side that we'll be able to figure out what we were learning and see why we picked some of the challenging themes or relationships in our lives.

— The next theme I want to address is that of the **Winner,** which is one you don't come across too often in life unless you run in the same circles as Donald Trump, Oprah Winfrey, Bill Gates, Tiger Woods, or Madonna. You don't only find them in the celebrity world because they can also live next door to you, but these names give you an idea of what the Winner is like. In its elevated form, as with the examples above, Winners are highly motivated against all odds. Unlike the Survivor, Winners have a definite goal in mind, and they're able to achieve it. In its lower form, it manifests itself in the kind of people who want another man's wife or woman's husband—just for the sake of saying that they're better and have won. They

can also sabotage fellow workers to get in the good graces of the boss.

The Winner can be more contrary than many themes. For example, when they're good, they're very, very good, but when they're bad, they're horrid. I've seen this many times, when one sibling will play the part of the good child and make the other one look bad just to win approval. It's truly wonderful to have the spirit of a Winner in all of us (like Spirituality)—but stepping on others or feeling the compulsion to win at all costs is a dangerous way to look at life.

Those with this theme do well with Activators, Catalysts, and Builders because they can be cheerleaders for each other.

⬧

It may seem that I've only given you the negative in this chapter, but I hope you'll see that if we extricate ourselves from challenging situations, we'll be left with a mate who's truly right for us and will bring us joy, rather than sorrow that ends in divorce. And regardless of what themes we have, we can get along with most of the others. As I've stated previously, however, this all depends on whether the other person has come to a spiritual understanding with their own themes. If they have, then those in most categories can make it together as spouses, friends, or family.

I've always felt that everyone should win, whether it's in a relationship or business deal or even at a dinner party. For instance, there's nothing more boring than listening to someone who can only discuss one subject, cause, or focus. No one wants to be consumed by any

one thing. Yes, we can put up with another's obsession, but not for long. I'm always baffled when people don't know that they're boring. They've got to see that our eyes have glazed over, we're fidgeting, or we're trying to keep from yawning. We have to be aware of this with our friends and loved ones and let them talk. We can be excited about something, but we need to allow them to vent or talk about their own problems or passions.

Too many relationships fail because just one person seems to carry the thread of communication and leaves the other silent because they feel that they have nothing to say or are too stupid to voice an opinion. If you're the dominant one in a relationship, you have to let the other person in, many times by simply asking, "What do you think?" It can be a good way of making this individual feel that his or her opinion is valid and worthwhile. Kindness and consideration are two of the most important factors in any relationship.

♕ ♕ ♕

Chapter Ten

A GOOD MATCH

efore I get back to the themes and how they relate to our relationships, I'd like to talk about homosexuality. Although same-sex partnerships are currently in the news, homosexuality has been around as long as humans have. It's not a by-product of modern society's ills, as many conservative churches or religious leaders would have us believe. Homosexuality is well documented in ancient civilizations, and many famous people throughout time have been same-sex oriented and have made great contributions to humankind. I think that we have to let people love whom they choose to love.

Many gays I know and truly adore aren't necessarily souls who've lived lives as a woman and then come into a male body or vice versa. When this does happen, though, guess what their predilection for a romantic relationship would be? Homosexuals often carry the themes of Experiencer or even Persecution or Victim. Much like the Jews in World War II, they've come to Earth to wake up the world to the horrors of bigotry.

Society's outcry against gays and their right to marry (fueled, as always, by religion) is ridiculous. Love is love, so why should we care who people are with as long as love is present? The sacrament of marriage is a commitment between two individuals who love each other. Religion should concentrate on the *commitment* and *love* parts, especially with the rising divorce rates, not on the gender of those wanting to marry.

Themes That Fit Well Together

Returning to the themes, I'd like to spend this chapter focusing on those that can fit very well together. Now you don't have to go around and wonder what everybody's theme is before you decide on a mate or relationship. Again, I'm only trying to give you a more detailed map of our learning process to show you why you do or don't get along with other people. I'll bet, though, that after you've read about the themes in more detail, you'll begin to understand why you hit it off like gangbusters with some people, while you simply can't deal with others at all.

— An **Experiencer** works well with the Activators or even the Catalysts. The latter are what I call "the Alka-Seltzer that makes the water bubble," and they get things done—maybe not as avidly as the Activator does, but the two have much in common.

— The **Banner Carrier** and **Cause Fighter** go well together. The Banner Carrier is seen picketing and demonstrating against injustice, sometimes focusing on too *many* injustices, while the Cause Fighter will stand with you and physically or verbally go toe-to-toe against any cause they feel passionate about. My dear friend Linda is a Cause Fighter, and if I were to ever be cornered, I'd want her at my side. Cause Fighters also go very well with the Justice theme.

— Like so many of the "people" themes, **Healers** have to take great care that they don't assimilate the illness they're trying to cure. It's very important for these individuals to protect themselves with "mental mirrors" that absorb negativity and to surround themselves and those they're working on with the white light of the Holy Spirit.

Most people in the medical or especially holistic areas of endeavor have this theme. For those who do their healing with the laying on of hands, it's especially effective when their relationship with the person to be healed is pure. Healers should never use their own energy, but just be a tube for God's energy to come through. The Psychic theme goes well with this one.

— **Intellectuality** is one of the themes that appeal to me more than good looks or anything else. I find those who use their minds to read, research, and explore truly sexy. Charles Darwin, Stephen Hawking, and Jonas Salk—all of whom used their research to help humankind—really perfected this theme. Those with the Intellectuality theme can get along quite well with Loners, Humanitarians, and Activators.

— The theme of **Leader** is a very interesting one. Although those with this theme aren't as innovative as Activators, they're very forward thinking and will take on the mantle of leadership. This theme goes well with the Follower or the Experiencer because the former keeps the Leader in charge, and the latter brings some excitement to their lives, especially since Leaders have a tendency to become workaholics if they don't have a diversion.

— As in astrology, some themes work better in the female than the male and vice versa. For example, the theme of **Warrior** fits better in the male. I don't mean that women can't be one, but they tend to be more gentle. My sons, for instance, both have this theme (they're rabid about providing for their families and protecting their homes), but so does my granddaughter, Angelia. She's very female, but she can't wait until she grows up so that she can save all the animals and go to Washington to tell them how to fix the tax laws.

These souls are often the risk takers and can assume many physical challenges. General George Patton typified this theme to the ultimate when he declared: "God, I love war!" Not every Warrior is in the military, but you can see these individuals in action in their protection of anyone they love. I feel that this theme is innate in so many males who don't have much to defend anymore.

Those with the Activator, Harmony, and Peacemaker themes temper the fire of the Warrior and make a very good match.

— I've always said that we need **Perfectionists** to get the job done right in this world. It's true, though, that there must be moderation in all things. The challenge of this theme is to stop believing that they're the only ones who know how things should be done.

They do very well with the Harmony theme because those individuals can calm the Perfectionist down. Those with the Patience and Tolerance themes can also be a good match, for they realize that's just the way the Perfectionist operates.

I'm going to end this chapter on a slightly different tack by talking about the **Psychic** theme in depth. While this theme is just what it seems—being able to see what others can't—many people find it strange that I don't have it. That's because psychic is what I *am*, not what I'm perfecting. One who has this theme may be a medium, be clairvoyant and/or clairaudient, do remote viewings, do healings, and be telekinetic; and although most have one or more of these abilities, I don't know of anyone who has had them all. For example, I freely admit that I'm not a physical medium and therefore do not have telekinetic powers.

As with any theme, souls who take on this one must use it wisely . . . realizing that they're only a tube by which knowledge from God, the Other Side, and their chart is obtained. This ability can also occur at any time—for example, Edgar Cayce came to it later in his life, while Peter Hurkos supposedly acquired the ability after falling off a ladder. In addition, people with the Psychic theme seem to come to it rather reluctantly because they feel that they're not normal and therefore want to negate it. (I came into my ability at birth, and although I did struggle with it, there was such a long history of psychics in my family that it helped me use this gift with God's help and for the right motives.)

If it isn't elevated, people with this theme might become so-called fortune-tellers who will tell you that you have a curse on you. They have some knowledge to catch you, but they use this as a hook. No psychic is 100 percent correct, and when people tell you that they'll give you a message if you just send them some money . . . run. It's highly illegal, not to mention morally wrong.

There are some great psychics out there, but unfortunately they (as well as myself at times) get overshadowed by these charlatans. As legitimate psychics, we have to continually fight the stigma that such fakers leave as their legacy. We're seeing disreputable people more and more frequently in other fields, such as religion, medicine, law, and business. Thanks to some outrageous scandals and the immediate impact of the media, today it seems as if we're battling corruption left and right. For some reason, however, psychics are not only viewed as being suspect by government and business watchdogs (which is fine by me), but we're also attacked by skeptics and religious organizations . . . many times without cause or reason. Ever since the age of Spiritualism, psychics have been grouped into the category of being possessed or in league with the devil, and thus labeled as "evil."

It's amazing to me that all through every religion, and especially in the Bible, prophets were revered, yet today they're attacked. Did God just up and say "No more prophets" one day? Did the psychic talent simply disappear from the earth? Are all the psychics today false prophets? Of course not! As I've said many times, we were all born with an ability to reach God, but somewhere along the way we dropped it or had it beaten out of us by society and religion. Well, the truth can be stomped on, attacked, and ridiculed, but it will still be there for all who want to see. Psychic ability is a fact and a reality, no matter what any organization or individual says. Look at how it's increasingly coming to the forefront with TV shows such as *Joan of Arcadia,* in which a teenager talked to God; and *Medium,* which is based on true events.

Now that it's somewhat permeating the world's consciousness, things are becoming easier, but you're always going to have the naysayers. In fact, relationships with skeptics can prove to be interesting lessons in how staunch you are in your beliefs. If someone can rattle you, no matter what profession you're in, you haven't arrived yet.

Recently I was on a TV show when a skeptic challenged me. Before he could get started, I asked if he believed in God. The reason I did so was because if he didn't have any spirituality, then there wouldn't be any platform we could meet on or even come to a place to agree to disagree. The man said that he didn't believe in God; and I've since learned that he allegedly failed to live up to his challenge in a test that he sent his representatives to observe and participate in, so what would be the point in adding to his own publicity? I also feel that dealing with him on TV was a waste of time that could have been better used to help someone in need.

I've been off the mark with some people (after all, no psychic is always correct), but I've been much more right than wrong, and countless individuals have been helped by my God-given gifts. I'm at a certain level of fame as a result of my abilities, so detractors will take their shots, but it really doesn't bother me anymore.

I've had many younger psychics tell me about bad publicity that has hurt them. I always reply, "If you're sure that what you're doing has a pure motive, then let the chips fall where they may. No one is here to win a popularity contest. These brief encounters can't get you down, because if you let people inspire self-doubt in you, then you're not committed to what you're doing. If you know that you can sleep at night and stand before God with your righteous motives, then it doesn't matter what anyone says. But if your motive and intent *aren't* spiritually driven, you won't fool people into thinking that they are."

Sometimes because of our beliefs, we have to take that leap and beat our own drum . . . it doesn't matter as long as our relationship with God never wavers. All else can fail us, but that never will. Consider what Christ went through—and all he taught was love. So if he can do it, why should we strive for any less? No, we're not him, but we can aspire to be like him.

I've been told by psychic medium John Edward that I tilled the field for those who came after me. I hope so . . . but I want it to be a field where the love of God thrives, too, not just barren earth. To that end, I tend to be extremely leery of any mediums who don't have a firm hold on God or the Christ consciousness or at least a strong spiritual base. I want to know what kind of lifestyle they have, if they're properly licensed to practice, and what organizations they support (if any). And while only God can be 100 percent correct, any psychic had better be significantly more right than wrong in the individual or overall scope. The scripted rhetoric offered by purported mediums on "psychic hotlines" relies on volume to make their businesses thrive, not accuracy.

Good psychics will have great track records and be in constant demand because of their accuracy, usually with a long wait before you can get an appointment with them and higher fees because of this demand. I know of some psychics who charge thousands of dollars for an individual reading. My fees are not cheap either ($700 to $800), but as I'm sure you know by now, I also help support three organizations, including a church, with these monies.

As an aside, I've often found that when I tell people something about their future in an individual reading, they contradict it down the road. People have a preconceived idea of what they want to hear, so if you don't tell them a particular thing, they'll oppose it. This doesn't bother me, for I know that the future more times than not pans out, and I've received many letters from those I've read for who've tried to negate something I told them would happen, only to have it happen anyway. I never blame them for this—after all, when my grandmother told me certain things about my future, I'd outwardly humor her but inwardly tell myself, *No way.*

"You will be a teacher" and "You will write and talk to thousands" were just a couple of things Grandma Ada told me about which I thought, *How crazy is that?* Well, it just goes to show you how much I knew about myself.

Oftentimes, those with the Psychic theme come from strict backgrounds where those in authority strive to suppress it. Hopefully they'll learn to live with their abilities and use them for good in a spiritual manner. People with this talent can also have a hard time with their mates because their partners don't understand the gift but keep their feelings bottled up—this is very hard and can put a strain on any relationship. The Emotionality theme would do well here because the psychic insight comes through the limbic (or emotional) brain. And the theme of Spirituality will understand that this entity is using their abilities for good rather than ego, fame, or fortune.

As I've mentioned, most themes in the long road to perfection and learning can connect with almost any other, especially if they're elevated to their highest spiritual level. But if the themes negate each other or the people don't live up to them (or at least try), then any and every relationship will fail.

👑 👑 👑

Chapter Eleven

HAPPILY EVER AFTER

$\mathcal{N}$ow that we've gone through our themes, which play such a significant part in our relationships, let's take a look at what everyone is interested in—our mates, significant others, lovers, or whatever name you want to give them.

I've often said that even though people are more interested in their spirituality than ever before, the number one question I'm asked is, "Where is Mr. or Ms. Right?" Well, having given readings for people for over 50 years, I've certainly noticed some patterns when it comes to finding "the One."

For those of you who are looking for a relationship or want to try to repair a current one, you must start by looking inside yourself. Begin with what you're *not* instead of what you *are*. In other words, you're (hopefully) not mean, deceptive, cruel, a liar, and so forth. When you've decided what you're not, then out of that cocoon of negativity comes the butterfly you wish to be.

Next, move on to what's good about yourself or even what you're aspiring toward—such as being kind, spiritual, loyal, grateful, committed, or what have you. This is your core essence, and it can help you determine what

would make a truly good relationship for *you*. You're now ready to attract many of the same qualities in another person that you respect and admire.

Always remember that we're here to learn. Sure, we all enjoy the heart-pounding throes of love's first flush, but are our partners people we can talk to? I'm not saying that looks aren't important, but they *are* pretty low on the list. Haven't we all known men or women who were physically attractive, yet the more we got to know them, the uglier they became? Those who rely on their appearance to take them through life are in a sad state because, like everything else, their looks will fade—but the soul's light never goes out.

I know that there have been tomes written about communication in relationships, but if we're comfortable with our partners, we don't have to talk all the time. Sometimes the quiet enjoyment of just being together, or having the security that the other person is beside us, is more than enough. There's also such a thing as talking too much, as the same song heard over and over again carries no weight. Screaming and yelling and calling each other names demeans you and the other person, while positive affirmations work every time. Appreciation, gratitude, and respect should take precedence in your relationship. After all, the concept of the Golden Rule is as old as time—ask yourself how *you'd* like to be called names, ignored, pushed away, or made to feel less than you are.

Being Genuine in a Relationship

We all have some preconceived notions of how love should be, which came from fairy tales, movies, and songs—we grow up with the constant reminder that love should be everlasting and perfect in every way, thus allowing us to ride off into the sunset and live happily ever after.

Then the reality of the world sets in. We meet people whose life themes are in a lower state or who have some deep-seated problems. But we can never find that perfect person because we're certainly not. Also, no one is entitled to total happiness . . . it must be earned. This may seem like a harsh statement, but too many people wrongly think that they deserve particular things in life. They do if they've worked for it, but not just because "I'm me." If we believe that, we're headed for doom. This doesn't mean that we don't deserve a good person who's highly evolved, especially if we've put in the time on ourselves.

No relationship is 100 percent perfect, but the *effort* of all parties involved better be 100 percent. Naturally your partner will be better at some things than others, but there are many ways in which you can make his or her life easier.

I also feel that so much has been written about relationships that we don't know which way to act anymore. In other words, if we feel that we have to behave in a certain way to please someone, then the mask of who we've become will slip at some point, whatever the other person thought we were won't be there anymore, and the relationship will fall apart.

The fear of rejection can make us act like what we think the other person wants—this can't last long, since keeping up such a pretense is exhausting. The rule is honesty (regardless of what your definition of that may be), to be yourself with all that you believe and are, and to put everything you are out in front. Then you'll be assured that you'll be loved for *you*, not someone you're only pretending to be.

One of the biggest keys to a successful relationship is to realize that it's not going to be perfect, so we can't let the world change us from who we really are. These days, for instance, men are programmed to have prostate problems, or women "go hormonal," so they don't care to make love anymore. My mother and father were still sexual with each other in their 80s because no one told them that they couldn't be (or if they did, it didn't sink in or take hold and make them impotent).

Making love isn't just for the propagation of children (which is important); rather, it means exactly what it states . . . to become *one* with your beloved. It's the sexual celebration of two bodies and souls coming together to form a singular being. In the initial heat of romance, everything seems to be perfect, until real life sets in—including jobs, finances, bills, children, births, deaths—causing passion to go out the proverbial window.

Yet if it's just sex that brings you together, you're in for disappointment. You can have fantastic intercourse with a person, but it's his or her essence that should be admired. Is your partner honest, ambitious, stable, committed, and loyal? Is he or she sensitive to your needs and emotions and then able to help you if necessary? How does your partner treat other people? If he or she is nice to you and cruel to others, then it's only a matter of time before it becomes your turn. Does this person respect you and your opinions, including your views on spirituality? These and many other questions should be asked before choosing a mate.

While we're on the subject of sex, I'd like to touch on sexual dysfunction, which can stem from myriad reasons. It can come from a feeling of violation or from the fear of giving or losing oneself, which often has little to do with the sexual act itself. It can even be from a past life that contained violence or rape, which comes with us as a morphic resonance of the past, or from a molestation in *this* life.

If making love has become a chore, then there are most likely other parts of life leaking into the bedroom. You can't be mean or quarrel in every other room and then expect that, once you're in the bedroom, everything will be all right. Criticism never works and can be a gut-punching way of getting a point across. "You don't help me in the way I'd like to be helped" is not criticism . . . it's a genuine cry for help. If you're working yourself senseless while your partner is just enjoying the fruits of your labor, it's not critical to say, "You have to help me hold up our lives instead of just lying around."

However, accusations such as "You spend too much!" "You never pay attention to me!" "We don't talk anymore!" or "It's not like it used to be!" *are* criticisms. The last statement is very important because nothing can ever stay the way it once was, and life takes us on a journey of change. Life is imperfect and messy—there's heartache, disappointment, anger, depression, financial problems, death, and challenges galore. Too many times when a relationship is tested, it crumbles. "Till death do us part" is wrong; instead, it should be, "I will be with you as a friend and helper for the rest of our lives."

Look at the wedding itself . . . take away the flowers, dresses, and reception, and it's a very serious religious ceremony, featuring a sacred vow made to each other and God. Then, for some reason, God and spirituality get lost, leaving us with no common religion or belief that we can rely on in something that's supposed to last a lifetime.

It does take two to break a relationship most of the time, but there are cases that can be exceptions. For example, we've chosen someone whom we truly believe has the same spiritual loyalty that we do, only to find out later that he or she was putting on an act. This then becomes a case of the other person breaking their vow or making a false one. All this boils down to the magnificent spiritual base that you want to build with your partner.

So many of my ministers are married, for instance, and not one of them has been divorced. It's not that Novus Spiritus is against it, but these ministers and their spouses are bound by their common beliefs and the knowledge that life is a journey of learning. We also provide spiritual counseling for each other and have no problem venting to each other and then meeting on common ground.

Now God knows that divorce can be inevitable due to circumstances. Of course you can't stay with someone who abuses you, cheats on you, or steals from you. But remember, just because you made a poor choice doesn't mean that you didn't live up to your vow. While the other person did break theirs, it's useless to be bitter about it. You can go on and love another day . . . hopefully smarter and more discerning in your choice of a mate.

The other thing I've seen in my readings is how many people keep repeating the same pattern. They marry the same type of person after a divorce—they may have different sizes or shapes, but they all share the same defective essence. That's when you have to take stock of yourself to determine why you keep picking such impossible relationships. Do you need to be punished or feel you must save someone? Such things need to be rectified before you can enjoy a healthy union. So find yourself—and your own essence that comes from God—and believe that you do deserve to be loved and respected.

The Truth about Soul Mates

I'd like to put the notion of soul mates in its proper and logical perspective once and for all. You see, souls have always been made in twos, like twins. As my spirit guide Francine says, "Each person as a created force was created in duality—male and female." In other words, there is another half of us, which almost always stays on the Other Side. Rarely does a soul mate incarnate with its twin soul, but we're so lucky to have other kindred souls whom we love deeply on Earth, such as our dear friends and loved ones, who are so important to us.

In fact, there are many people in this life (or others) who can mean as much to us as a soul mate does. As my psychic son, Chris, once told me many years ago, "Mom, I might have had other mothers in my past lives, but I know in my heart that I will always love you best." A child, parent, grandchild, or even a friend can be a true kindred soul, both here and at Home. After all, on the Other Side we aren't around just one person, abandoning all the other wonderful people we've ever known. In fact, Francine says that more times than not, we don't tend to hang around with our soul mate. Yes, there is a special relationship with our twin soul, but it's never the be-all and end-all of life.

I'm also not convinced that when Jesus said, "What God has joined together, let no man put asunder," he was only referring to marriage. I think he meant to cleave your intellect from your emotion. He was also referring to *all* relationships because here again, if you're not complete, no one will be able to be everything for you. That's why the soul-mate concept can be so misleading—especially since this soul almost always stays on the Other Side.

So the soul mate does make us feel complete, like finding the deeper understanding of ourselves. But as Francine says, souls will choose to be with or marry others when incarnate. We go through countless experiences, and sometimes one soul outgrows the other one (which also imitates life when one person grows and his or her partner stays stagnant). Of course these two are still connected—it's just that one has evolved to a greater degree than the other half has. This doesn't mean that your soul mate stops watching out for you or loving you—you two will be close for eternity. So instead of looking for the *one* soul mate, enjoy all the wonderful people you know and love here and from other lives . . . and even on the Other Side.

We all know when we meet a kindred, loving soul. If you keep looking for that perfect person, you're setting yourself up to fail, especially since *you're* not perfect. You hear that love conquers all—well, if you're in a giving, truly unconditional, respectful, and caring relationship, then it will.

Things Aren't Always as They Seem

Romantic relationships can be as diverse as anything we can imagine in life. We often judge by looks to see if certain people seem to fit together. So many times we hear, "What does she see in him?" I remember some years ago being acquainted with a couple, and he truly looked like a movie star while she appeared to be a "plain Jane." At first it was difficult to see the attraction, but after a while, I got it. Even with his great looks, he was very obsessive and insecure, while she was really bubbly and served as his anchor. So don't let what you see on the outside belie how the soul is underneath.

I was watching a show on TV recently and was amazed to hear that if let loose in the wild, after a few generations, domesticated pigs will revert back and become like their cousins, the wild boars. These feral hogs even grow bristly hair and tusks. How does this apply to our relationships? Well, sometimes the bad influences we're around can negatively impact us, so when we're seeking a mate, it's a good idea to see what kind of people surround this person. It may not seem fair, but we *are* judged by the company we keep. Birds of a feather do flock together, and if you're the odd bird out, you'll never fit in, no matter how hard you try. Sure, some people choose lives of addiction or despondency, but I've found that they're either dark or very new souls who are just too inexperienced to get it.

Dark entities have no guilt, are never wrong, and live in a world in which they're the only ones who matter. When you come into contact with such entities, run—there's no logical or spiritual reason why you should waste your time trying to "save" them. Christ said, "Don't cast your pearls before swine," so if he wouldn't, why should you? There are too many wonderful people who will value you and won't just want you around for what you can do for them. It's important to remember that all relationships need to have a give-and-take or they're simply not worth your while.

And although they say that opposites attract, my grandmother used to wisely come back with, "But similars stay together." Of course you don't want someone exactly like yourself, because although these individuals can be very captivating in the beginning—you like purple, and so do they; you like teddy bears, and they like them, too . . . on and on it goes—it's as if they've assumed your identity. This can be very flattering at first, but it can then become very aggravating. You might as well just live by yourself rather than being involved in such a parasitic relationship.

Psychology says that this behavior can result from having parents who were unapproachable; consequently, such individuals latch onto anyone whose personality they can assimilate in order to gain approval. I do believe that we chart things like this and can really learn from someone who's saddled with this type of personality. After all, no one wants to be a therapist or parent in their relationship . . . we all want an equal and balanced partnership.

You should never believe that there's anyone who's worth breaking your contract with God. There will be times when your heart is so broken that you feel as if you're going to die (or you wish you could), but your spiritual knowledge will keep you going . . . to live and love another day.

Sure, you picked your chart to learn, so you may very well say, "Well, if I already picked all this, then I can't change it." Of course you chose your life and its lessons, but just because there's a boulder in the road of your chart doesn't mean that it was written for you to just sit there on it. Go around it, or climb over it, so that you'll get to the better side of life and be happy. This is simply a test of spiritual strength.

The tests are written in our charts, but so is the ability to sustain or overcome them. We'll eventually get back on track, but sometimes we make ourselves suffer more than is needed. It's this world and the human condition (as Francine says) that makes us confused and even stupid. It's a wonder we aren't even *more* confused, what with coming into this hellhole with thousands of overlays of behaviors from past lives, plus all the programmed conditioning we see in movies, TV, books, and so forth.

More on Same-Sex Unions

Since we're on the subject of love and challenges, I want to talk a little more about an issue that very few people seem to want to address logically. Whether you are for or against same-sex relationships, I think that we should let people love whom they want and not question why. I remember once talking to a teacher of mine in college about love and literature, and she said, "I don't think it matters whom or what we love because God *is* love." And Jesus never once made any references to the subject of homosexuality—it only appears in the Old Testament because those men wanted the population to expand to get more members for their religion.

Many gay people have decided to incarnate in this way in order to enlighten people to love on all levels. For example, I have a dear male friend who's gay and has AIDS, yet he helps others and is an example to us all. He's so kind and caring, and he's been a great asset to me in my research and spirituality.

I've lost so many loved ones to AIDS that my blood boils whenever I hear prejudiced and mean-spirited remarks. This kind of bigotry can make it very difficult to be tolerant, and I always think, *Be careful what you hate, for you might find yourself coming back into life as the very thing you despise. So live and let live or you might find yourself living that type of life.*

It seems that when a particular cause begins to infringe on people's freedom to love whom they want to, or to live a different but lawful lifestyle, then that cause is setting itself up as judge and jury. I don't remember reading that Jesus put anyone in charge to be an advocate for prejudice and bigotry, or to tell us whom we can or can't love.

This type of thinking can even leak over to different types of prejudice, such as a person of color loving a Caucasian, or members of different ethnic groups or religions being together. I find it amusing that when we get to the Other Side, we can share essences or merge with anyone and nobody cares what sex we are. It's just souls sharing love with other souls.

The more spiritual you become, realizing that there's nothing new under God's sun, the more you'll understand that everyone makes up the different chords in a larger symphony that should play in harmony, not discord. Why should we make relationships so hard— whether due to age, color, race, creed, time, or space? I also wonder why we don't spend more time enjoying each other rather than picking each other apart.

◄◦►

Ingredients for a Successful Relationship

To have a successful relationship of any kind requires several basic ingredients that some people might not even realize. First of all, you must have a good dose of spirituality. Many do not understand the terms *spiritual* or *spirituality,* for they tend to attach them to religion in one form or another. In actuality, although religion might help or deter you in the process of becoming spiritual, you don't have to practice a faith to be a successfully spiritual person. In other words, religion doesn't necessarily have anything to do with being a good person! To be perfectly clear, to be spiritual is nothing more than *trying to be the best possible person you can be and doing your best for God.*

We're all human, and we all make mistakes or even fail sometimes. A pure motive negates the mistakes and failures, while having an impure or ulterior motive augments them. In other words, while getting married just because you love someone carries a pure motive, doing so because someone has a lot of money isn't so pure. The key component of any pure motive is love, just as love is the key component of life. To do something out of love is the purest of motives, while to do something for your own gain is not so pure. I could go on and give hundreds of examples of a pure motive as opposed to an impure motive, but I think you get the point.

Whenever you do something with an impure motive, the natural by-product is guilt (unless you're just a dark-souled person), because it's directly related to your conscience. At one time or another, all of us have experienced a pang of remorse because we did something we weren't proud of with an impure motive . . . again, because we're human and have human emotions, it happens. If we continue to engage in actions that produce guilt, and with a motive to do so, our level of spirituality drops; but if we do something that hurts someone, but we *didn't* have the intent to do so, our level won't drop. For example, getting into an automobile accident that causes harm to others may cause guilt, but the motive wasn't there to harm anyone. But if you run somebody off the highway because of road rage, then the intent to harm is there because you lost your temper.

We all have faults, and to become better human beings we not only have to recognize them but work to overcome them. The way to become a better person is to learn to love unconditionally and practice tolerance.

To love unconditionally means to emanate love without any thought of something coming back to you for your own gain. We often see this in everyday life with parents loving their children even though they may not be the best little boys or girls. One of the by-products of unconditional love is true forgiveness; for when we love unconditionally, we don't place conditions on our feelings, so we can truly forgive the transgressions of those we care about. In order to be better human beings, we should try to love as much and as many as we can without any thought of reward. Love should be free and flowing, not restricted by conditions. The great thing about love is that even though you should love without thought of reward, if you send it out, love will invariably come back to you through God's universal law of "what you put out comes back to you."

People are always looking for hard-and-fast rules for finding a mate or staying married (and there are none), but no one seems to place any emphasis on just the love of self. A friend of mine and I, for instance, don't have spouses, but we get manicures and pedicures and our hair done—for *us*. Even if I'm sick, I have to bathe, change my nightgown, and brush my teeth and hair. It doesn't matter that I'm the only one who's going to see me.

Although life crowds in, I don't advocate letting ourselves go after we're settled in a relationship. "Love me the way I am" is one thing, but to walk around in a dirty robe and with greasy hair for a week isn't very appealing to anyone—this shows that you don't respect yourself or the other person. Gaining a little weight (I said "a little") is fine, for to be happy in your own skin is great, but to become obese can not only be a detriment to your health but also to your self-esteem.

Sometimes when you and your partner bond together, you can diet, break habits, and support each other in all things. I've said that spirituality isn't just praying; it's caring, loving, and being kind and considerate. This is what it means to follow the teachings of Christ (or similar tenets). To live with goodness is following the purpose that God put you here for and why you chose to come here to learn.

Then again, that expression "You can never be too rich or too thin" makes my blood boil because it overlooks some important aspects of self, such as confidence and spirituality. And running out and having every plastic-surgery procedure that's open to us is also a little much. Sure, I've had laser resurfacing and a Botox injection here and there, but I also want to look my age and grow older gracefully. Not long ago a friend and I were sitting

in a restaurant in Los Angeles, and we kept watching these blonde women coming down from the upstairs with marked interest. They all looked exactly alike—so "pulled" that they appeared to be on a motorcycle going 100 miles an hour with bugs in their teeth. My friend and I both said, "Let's leave just in case it's catching!" As we went outside, we looked up to see that a plastic surgeon's office was above the restaurant.

Again, if something's really affecting your life—for example, if it's difficult to breathe through your nose or you have no chin or whatever, then by all means get it done *if you want to.* But altering yourself just because you fear that your spouse will leave you for someone who's younger and better looking is only going to leave you disappointed. Have you ever thought about what a young, taut face would look like on an old body? It would be as if you'd had your head transplanted on another body or vice versa. If you don't have enough confidence to explore your own self and be aware of your spouse's inner beauty, then no amount of fixing the exterior will help.

The actress Billie Burke (who played Glinda, the "good witch," in *The Wizard of Oz*) was married to theatrical producer Florenz Ziegfeld, Jr., and it's said that she'd get up a half an hour before him to put on makeup and "look pretty" when he awoke. I guess she was insecure about all the beautiful girls he was surrounded by in his line of work, but they did stay together until he died. I doubt it was only because she always had her makeup on around him, but rather because they respected each other. She also tried very hard to show him that she cared (even though all that effort seems exhausting), and he must have appreciated it.

Now one thing that seems unbelievably unfair to me is the attitude about taking a younger spouse. You see, if the male is older, it doesn't seem to matter; in fact, he's hailed as quite a stud. But if a woman does it, she's a "cradle robber." Look at Demi Moore, Celeste Holm, or Martha Raye—people can be so critical of females who choose a younger mate, but I say, if it makes two people happy, then let them be. Soul recognizes soul, as I've said; and age, time, culture, and color aren't barriers when one soul connects to another spiritually.

How do you know if you've made a connection on a soul level? First of all, you have to give it time—rushing into anything, especially a lifelong commitment such as marriage, is foolish. Then you need to explore each other's likes and dislikes, financial goals, and spiritual beliefs. Notice that I didn't mention one thing about religious preference because true spirituality meets on a higher, more rational plateau.

While we're on the subject, I find it so sad that if two people have a happy marriage, they can be in for some big-time jealousy. It's so awful, but spouses in other marriages will ask each other, "Why can't you be more like Helen?" "Why can't you be the type of husband that Bill is?" or "Their marriage is perfect—why can't *we* have one like that?" This is a deadly one-way street. If you're feeling this way, try to remember why you married this person. Of course he or she has changed, but so have you. So instead of being jealous of someone else's happiness, try telling your spouse, "I'm glad I married you instead of someone else." It also goes a long way toward healing old ills and misspoken words.

There's Always Joy in Life

Whether we're in a romantic partnership or not, life gives us lost loves, disappointing family members, the empty-nest syndrome (except in my case, thank God), hormonal changes, infidelities, aloneness, depression, death, illness, loss of friendships, career deflations, moves, and financial problems. But it also gives us children and grandchildren, loving pets, friends who stay and laugh together, and myriad other blessings. We derive comfort from knowing that we'll see our loved ones who have passed on. We mature and realize that we don't need as much as we thought. We have friends who are true and people we love.

Someone once said to me, "But if you're not married, Sylvia, you'll die alone." In the first place, no one dies alone. We're *born* alone, but dying is returning Home to a party with our loved ones. I've had three marriages, and just because they didn't work out doesn't mean that I was left bitter and alone. Instead, I learned a lot about myself, such as the fact that I'm really not psychic about myself or my romantic partners. Also, many men would find it hard to live with me and my absorption with my family. In addition, my schedule is a tough one to get used to—I'm traveling, writing, doing readings, helping with police cases, doing Montel's show, answering letters, assisting my ministers, and doing pro-bono work; plus I run a corporation, a church, several study groups and salons, and on it goes. So where would a relationship fit in, and how unfair would that be to both of us?

So you pick your road, your goals, and your future in life, and hopefully you've learned from the past and will be happy with all that you have until you go Home. As for me, I live in my own place, but I'm only about ten minutes away from all of my family members. Sure I work hard, but I love what I do and the people I see and read for. At age 70, I move a little more slowly, but I still seem to wear most people out. I don't have a husband, but I do have wonderful male friends and a dear male companion. I don't want to get married again, but I celebrate everyone who wants to. I've done the marriage thing, and now I have another focus for the love in my life: my family, God, and all of you.

Will I retire? Never! We're not a family who retires—my father worked with me until he was 85, my mother taught until she was almost 80, and my grandmother was still doing readings at age 88. I'm convinced that if you stop, you die. And why would you want to stop? Why go to Disneyland and only take one ride? Auntie Mame said that "life is a banquet!" so why not try a little bit of everything? It will make you learn more, keep you younger and more alert, and give you a feeling of accomplishment for God.

All the good things in life combine with the hard knocks to bring us experience and knowledge. I've been criticized, impugned, lied about, defamed, disliked, and perhaps even hated by some people, yet all of it has made me a better and wiser person. I will never back down from my beliefs or compromise my integrity, no matter what anyone says about me. I know what I know, I know what I believe, I know my God, and I know that I'll continue to try to help as many people as I can with the gifts I've been given.

Life becomes a montage of strength and joy if you just use your talents to help others. By bonding together and sharing what you know, you won't feel so alone. So

stop wringing your hands over any supposed failures or so-called guilt and pick yourself up and fill your life with the love that waits for you at every turn. Try to remember the good times, and look to your loved ones for support. And when you feel down and want to have a "pity party," remember that wherever there's a hole left in life, if you open your heart . . . God will fill it up.

♕ ♕ ♕

Afterword

*T*here are self-help books out there that may give you some guidance in preparing for matrimony, and others that may help you if you're already married, so I wanted to end this book a little differently by giving you a list of the all-time worst reasons to get married. There's only one true reason to wed, and that's love—so if you're doing it for any of the reasons listed below, your chances for a successful union are slim to none.

Don't Get Married If . . .

1. You want to get away from home.

2. You're afraid that you won't find anyone else.

3. Everyone else is doing it . . . so why not you?

4. You said yes to the first person who asked you because you don't want to end up a bachelor or an old maid.

5. People will feel that there's something wrong with you if you don't wed.

6. You desire financial security.

7. Your family is pressuring you into marriage.

8. You feel that you'll always be a third wheel if you remain single.

9. You just want to have children.

Let's break each one of these down.

1. You want to get away from home. So many young people want to leave their parents' homes and face the world, but getting married shouldn't be the catalyst. It's better to move into your own place first—get a roommate if necessary, or even live with your significant other before jumping into something like marriage just to escape. We should always run *toward* something, not *away*.

2. You're afraid that you won't find anyone else. This one is just ridiculous. If you genuinely want to get married, then chances are that it's in your chart. You'll find someone else if your estimation of self and your spirituality are intact, for you'll believe that you're capable of loving and being loved. Don't sell yourself short—your wares certainly belong in a good market.

3. Everyone else is doing it . . . so why not you? Where is it written that love has to be found by a certain age? If you look around, you'll see just how many people have made this very mistake. It's better to find a good person who makes you happy at age 50 than settle for someone at age 20 who makes you miserable—and will continue to do so for years to come.

4. You said yes to the first person who asked you because you don't want to end up a bachelor or an old maid. This can be a cultural determinism, as some women in India and other countries marry before they can even menstruate. Years ago, most women got married in their teens, which had much to do with the fact that life spans were so short—even as recently as 100 years ago, many people didn't reach 40 years of age. Feeling as if "everyone else is doing it, so if I don't I'll be left behind" or "I'll miss out on something" is just the voice of fear talking. You must never compromise your ethics or what you want from a partner. Again, it's better to have no marriage than be in one that's terribly unhappy.

5. People will feel that there's something wrong with you if you don't wed. Yes, some individuals may think or say hateful things if you're not married, but look to see where they're coming from. Is their life that happy, or are they jealous of your single status? If you keep to your own goals and set your standards high enough to meet your expectations—especially what you need from a companion, lover, and spiritual confidant—love will come to you.

6. You desire financial security. To marry for financial security is really stupid because it negates the whole purpose of matrimony. I cannot imagine committing to a person you don't love, but if you do, you'll find out very quickly that your life is empty. After all, marriage is a union of love, not convenience. Money can't buy happiness, only things—so if that's all you marry for and the relationship goes south, then what do you do? Sure, you might be able to get a settlement, but how empty would that be?

If money is what you want, get it through a career. Finding your own financial security will lift your self-esteem greatly. Also, to live by your chart means that you take some responsibility for your own worth as a human being. The impure motive of marrying for money will certainly not reap rewards in your spirituality.

7. Your family is pressuring you into marriage. When I was 18, my grandmother on my father's side was constantly on my case to get married and start a family; whereas on my mother's side, women didn't get married until their 30s, and they had children even later (my mother had me at 42 and my sister at 48), which was very progressive at that time. My father's mother was all for early marriages, while Grandma Ada's philosophy was "Take your time . . . you're making a moral and spiritual commitment for life." There's no set schedule for marriage—if it's meant to happen, it will when it's supposed to. As I've said so many times, you always follow your chart, like it or not.

8. You feel that you'll always be a third wheel if you remain single. No, you won't. If you have your own ideas, keep up with the world, and are friendly and kind, you'll be someone whom others want around. In fact, when I was married the first time, I went to so many places without my husband that many people didn't even know I was married. How many couples do you know where you're entranced by one and don't really care about the other because he or she is just a quiet, remote fixture? I'm not saying that you or your spouse has to be the life of the party, but being married doesn't identify you in any special way . . . your soul does.

9. You just want to have children. Again, this is a situation where the reason for marriage is self-serving rather than based on love. In this day and age, it's also completely unnecessary to marry to have children—there are so many single parents today because of divorce and the increasing number of unmarried individuals who are also having or adopting kids. There are sperm banks and surrogate mothers out there, as well as a large number of orphans who need loving homes. You don't have to commit to an unwanted union just to have children—if you do, the chances of your family being unhappy just increase dramatically.

―◄◊►―

Children are an essential part of most marriages, and many people want them in their lives, but what about the individual who doesn't want any? Since I gave you some reasons why you shouldn't marry, I thought it would also be beneficial to list some of the worst reasons to have kids.

You Shouldn't Have Children
If You Think That . . .

1. It will save your marriage.
2. Everyone else is having them, so you should, too.
3. People will see you as selfish.
4. You really don't want to be a father or mother.

Again, let's go through the list one by one.

1. It will save your marriage. This is probably one of the worst reasons to have a baby. There are a million reasons to bring a child into the world, but one of them shouldn't be to glue something that's already been broken. If your relationship is on the rocks, a kid won't save it; if anything, it will exaggerate your problems and make things worse. One or both partners may also feel left out or even trapped. Children are God's blessings, but they need a lot of time and care. If they're brought into an already unhappy home, this hurts everyone—especially the innocent babes.

2. Everyone else is having them, so you should, too. This is cut from the same cloth as "Everyone else is married, so I should, too," except this one is more serious. This is a precious life that we're talking about here—one that's yours forever and that you're responsible for. This isn't just some add-on that automatically comes with marriage (although when the setting is right, it's perfect and everyone wins). Check your motive, and if it's pure, then go ahead and have a baby. But don't do it because you feel left out . . . a child is not a commodity, but a living, breathing soul entrusted to your care by God.

3. People will see you as selfish. Here we go again with the cultural norms. If you're worried about how you're appearing to other people, then please don't have children. And if you don't feel that you can handle kids, then it's far more selfish to have them than to abstain. The child won't benefit, and believe me, he or she will sense your resentment.

4. You really don't want to be a father or mother. There are many people who love children, but they know at an early age that they'd rather not have any of their own. This is perfectly all right. I know a lot of people who don't have children and are happy, and people who have them and aren't happy. Sometimes this comes from a past life (as so many things do) in which we had many children, so we don't want to do it again in this life. Whatever your reasons are, if you follow your own spiritual feelings, you'll never go wrong.

At one time I was convinced that I was going to be a nun. I went so far as to be accepted by two orders—the Franciscans and Saint Joseph of Carondelet—but then I began to think about how I'd always wanted children. So even though I was torn for a while, I opted for marriage and children (although I still can't hear a Gregorian chant without getting a lump in my throat). It was charted to be . . . even though I had four miscarriages before Paul. As he later told me one day when he was about two, "Boy, Mom, it sure took me a long time to get here."

I then had three more miscarriages after Chris came along. In those days there was no fertility science to speak of, and one doctor finally caught that my production of

thyroid hormones was extremely low. So, yes, having my boys was hard, but what was to be came about, and I fulfilled my chart.

As far as romantic partners go, Grandma Ada used to say that finding the right person was like picking cotton—some tufts are white and pure, while others look all right but are full of boll weevils (the bugs that infest cotton). I'm sure we've all picked what we felt was a pure cotton ball only to find out that it had more bugs or flaws than we could live with. Yet it's the act of picking that's important—if it doesn't go so well, that's not necessarily our fault.

So no matter what you go through in life, as long as you have your hand in God's, you're ahead of the game. And while there are no hard-and-fast rules for being happy, if you surround yourself with your loved ones, you'll be truly blessed.

Look around at your gardener, manicurist, butcher, mechanic, and all the other people who are in your life . . . they're parts of a wonderful montage of love and light. Each person you meet adds to this light, and it gets brighter each time you give out love and caring to one another.

You don't have to holler down a well or scream in the mountains just to get your own voice to echo back the words *I love you.* Everywhere you look, there are people to love and spiritually connect to . . . which is all part of God's plan.

God love you. I do. . . .
— *Sylvia*

✠ ✠ ✠

ABOUT THE AUTHOR

Sylvia Browne is the #1 *New York Times* best-selling author and world-famous psychic medium who appears regularly on *The Montel Williams Show* and *Larry King Live,* as well as making countless other media and public appearances. With her down-to-earth personality and great sense of humor, Sylvia thrills audiences on her lecture tours and still has time to write numerous immensely popular books. She has a master's degree in English literature and plans to write as long as she can hold a pen.

Sylvia is the president of the Sylvia Browne Corporation; and is the founder of her church, the Society of Novus Spiritus, located in Campbell, California. Please contact her at: **www.sylvia.org**, or call **(408) 379-7070** for further information about her work.

ψ ψ ψ

NOTES

NOTES

Hay House Titles of Related Interest

DAILY GUIDANCE FROM YOUR ANGELS:
365 Angelic Messages to Soothe, Heal, and Open Your Heart,
by Doreen Virtue, Ph.D.

EVERYTHING YOU NEED TO KNOW TO FEEL GO(O)D,
by Candace B. Pert, Ph.D.

FOUR ACTS OF PERSONAL POWER:
How to Heal Your Past and Create a Positive Future,
by Denise Linn

HEALING YOUR FAMILY HISTORY:
5 Steps to Break Free of Destructive Patterns,
by Rebecca Linder Hintze

THE HEART OF LOVE:
How to Go Beyond Fantasy to Find True Relationship Fulfillment,
by Dr. John F. Demartini

INSPIRATION: *Your Ultimate Calling,*
by Dr. Wayne W. Dyer

POWER OF THE SOUL: *Inside Wisdom for an Outside World,*
by John Holland

PRACTICAL SPIRITUALITY,
by John Randolph Price

RECLAIM YOUR SPIRITUAL POWER,
by Ron Roth, Ph.D., with Peter Occhiogrosso

TOUCHING THE DIVINE:
How to Make Your Daily Life a Conversation with God (book-with-CD),
edited and interpreted by Gay Hendricks and James Twyman

YOUR IMMORTAL REALITY:
How to Break the Cycle of Birth and Death,
by Gary R. Renard

All of the above are available at your local bookstore,
or may be ordered by contacting Hay House (see last page).